THE MEDICAL CARE SYSTEM

A Conceptual Model

THE MEDICAL CARE SYSTEM

A Conceptual Model

Michael J. Long

AUPHA Press/Health Administration Press
Ann Arbor, Michigan   1994

98 97 96 95 94   5 4 3 2 1

Library of Congress Cataloging-in-Publication Data

Long, Michael J.
   The medical care system : a conceptual model / Michael J. Long.
      p.   cm.
   Includes bibliographical references and index.
   ISBN 1-56793-016-6 (alk. paper : softbound)
   1. Medical economics.   2. Medical care.   I. Title.
   [DNLM: 1. Health Services—organization & administration—United States.
2. Health Services—supply & distribution—United States.   3. Health Services
Needs and Demand—United States.   4. Social Values.   W 84 AA1 L84m
1994]   RA410.L66   1994   338.4'33621—dc20   94-34492 CIP

The paper used in this publication meets the minimum requirements of American National Standard for Information Sciences—Permanence of Paper for Printed Library Materials, ANSI Z39.48-1984. ∞™

Health Administration Press
A division of the Foundation
   of the American College of
   Healthcare Executives
1021 East Huron Street
Ann Arbor, Michigan 48104
(313) 764-1380

Association of University Programs
   in Health Administration
1911 North Fort Myer Drive, Suite 503
Arlington, VA 22209
(703) 524-5500

This book is dedicated to the memory of my son Adrian.

Contents

Foreword

Nothing delights the heart of an aging professor so much as seeing how his former students blossom and bear fruit. He can claim some credit for the seed he has sown and the early nurture of the tender plant, but thereafter, he can only watch at a distance and marvel at the results.

It is with a sense of paternal satisfaction, therefore, that I introduce this book by Michael J. Long. It is a work outstanding in many respects.

It is notable for using a single, unifying model which allows systematic, stepwise development of the subject. It takes pains to offer numerous examples by means of which abstract concepts become more concrete, comprehensible, and persuasive. And it is remarkable for the lucidity and precision of the language with which it speaks. Add to all this the consistency and coherence that only authorship by a single scholar can give, and you have a remarkable contribution indeed.

This is an exposition easily accessible to the beginner, but it is also inclusive and sound enough to be a firm foundation for subsequent specialization. Even the more advanced student could learn from the organizing framework by which, in this work, factual material is organized and rendered more meaningful.

For all these reasons, I bid this book Godspeed and wish it success.

Avedis Donabedian
Ann Arbor, 1994

Preface

The medical care organization field is replete with many texts that, with few exceptions, tend to address, albeit piecemeal, the various constructs and issues generally accepted as the relevant ones. This approach results in a series of chapters, each dealing with a particular concept or issue with no attempt to tie the work together in a meaningful way. In contrast, it has been my experience, having taught a variety of undergraduate and graduate students in two countries, that students require the pedagogical process to be as conceptual as possible to render it generalizable. Typically, a rigorous medical care organization course draws on materials from many sources, both texts and journal articles, with the instructor's syllabus serving as the framework for integrating the material. The framework is often little more than a personal ordering preference, with perhaps more than just a little of "this is how it was taught to me" thrown in. As a result, students complete the course with some understanding of the independent concepts and issues but with no real grasp of the overall system. In other words, they have been given all the component parts without a set of assembly instructions.

One outstanding exception to this approach is Dr. Avedis Donabedian's classic work *Aspects of Medical Care Administration: Specifying Requirements for Health Care* (1973), a systematic examination of the existing medical care literature through the early 1970s. As a student of Donabedian's, I was fortunate enough to be exposed to his work and writings firsthand—an experience that not only endowed me with an enthusiasm for the subject that prevails still today, but that also provided me with a blueprint for how to teach my own students.

My teaching responsibilities have brought me into contact with baccalaureate and graduate students in nontraditional and traditional programs in the United States and Canada. Many of those students came to the field with a clinical background. As imperative as it seems to me that they understand the approach taken by Donabedian, their backgrounds and their outside commitments have made the process of facilitating such an understanding quite a challenge. It has required that I further systematize an already systematic approach and to reinterpret some of the esoteric material.

This book is, therefore, intended as an introductory text for senior baccalaureate and first-year graduate students in academic and professional degree programs in the health care field. It is equally appropriate for health administration, medical, and allied health students.

It is expected that an instructor using this text would supplement it with current journal articles and the appropriate chapters from other well-established texts in the field.

Donabedian, in the preface of his aforementioned book, recognizes the occasional difficulty in attributing the contributions of the appropriate people to any literary work. This is particularly so with this text. Having been a student of Donabedian's and thoroughly indoctrinated as a willing, enthusiastic fellow traveler, it is impossible to identify to what extent original thought prevails. Quite apart from this concern, the very objective of this book—a logical, smoothly flowing conceptual model of the medical care system—would be destroyed if every other sentence carried a reference notation. Perhaps the most ethical solution to this dilemma would be to credit Donabedian with the entire contents of this book. However, this would have the effect of holding him responsible for inadequacies that may appear here—inadequacies that are mine alone. Instead, I would prefer to acknowledge the contribution he has made to my education and academic career.

The contents of this book can fill one semester with the aid of supplementary material. I recommend instructors follow the order of presentation. Chapter 1 places the medical care system in context and distinguishes between health care and medical care. Because the medical care system is considered in the context of the economic system, the implications of different perspectives on the use of medical care can be discussed. Key to this approach is recognizing medical care as an input (to health) *and* as an output ("more is better"). Chapter 1 leads naturally into Chapter 2's discussion of how social values influence the medical care system, which facilitates an understanding of our current system and its component parts.

In Chapter 3, the conceptual model of the medical care system is presented, which is briefly explained to introduce the terminology. The model is the heart of the book, from which all that follows emanates.

Chapters 4 and 5 demonstrate how to determine the number and type of medical care services required to address the need for care that has been identified. Chapters 6, 7, and 8 provide an understanding of how to arrive at the number and type of medical care services available.

Access, covered in Chapter 9, is identified as the meshing of the supply-side and demand-side characteristics. Once access is achieved, results of utilization and the extent to which need is addressed can be determined, which is discussed in Chapter 10.

Finally, Chapter 11 examines the generalizability and utility of the conceptual model by discussing various types of medical care service and by identifying the point of impact in the model of specific legislative interventions. In this manner, all implications can be considered by tracing the effect throughout the system.

Instructors may find that more than one week is required to cover some chapters. I have found that one week is not always enough to cover the material presented in Chapters 1 and 9, but most semesters can still accommodate an 11-chapter text.

Chapter 1

The Context of Medical Care

This chapter will discuss the difference between health care and medical care. Because this book addresses medical care the term must be precisely defined so that it is not ambiguous in the mind of the reader. Understanding this material will be greatly enhanced by recognizing the muddled thinking and sloppy terminology that has unfortunately gained acceptance and led to many misunderstandings.

The distinction between health care and medical care having been made, the place of the medical care system in the economic system will be considered. While any social system might be examined from a variety of perspectives, the economic model can be justified for at least two important reasons: First, medical care is a service predominantly delivered in the private sector so is therefore subject to many of the attendant concerns and implications of such an economic transaction. Second, use of the economic model permits consideration of the relationship between personal health and economic health.

An economic approach brings to light the input-output chain relationship that leads to discussing the effects of viewing medical care as an input to health or as an end in and of itself, as an output. This latter view has considerable implications on the concept of marginal improvement in health status and provides the catalyst for a discussion of "flat of the curve" medical care.

Finally, this chapter extends the concepts of marginal contribution to health status and the input-output considerations to include a brief study of the difficulty in measuring outcomes of the medical care system.

Health Care and Medical Care

How often is it said that health care costs are "too high," or "rising too rapidly"? These are truisms that would meet with no dissenters. Generally speaking, however, those who make such statements are not referring to health care, and more often than not, they are not even referring to the costs. To understand what is meant by *health care costs* requires understanding what is meant by *health care*.

Consider that in most sectors of the economy, there is no ambiguity when discussing a product's costs. For example, we understand what is meant by automobile costs and movie ticket costs because discussions of these subjects are reasonably well defined and fairly sharply focused. This is not the case with health care, where it has become the rule rather than the exception to use health care synonymously for *medical care*. Just as it is incorrect to consider movies the sole component of the entertainment industry, it is incorrect to consider medical care the sole component of the health care industry. In both of these examples, the components are necessary but not sufficient to define the industry or sector of which they are a vital part. If health care is not synonymous with medical care, what is meant by health care and where does medical care fit into the scheme of things?

To understand these terms better, let's consider how health is defined. The World Health Organization (WHO) defines health as something more than the absence of disease. It is, according to WHO, a state of complete physical, mental, and social well-being (World Health Organization 1958; Somers and Somers 1977). This definition is noteworthy because it includes measures other than physical well-being.

Many other attempts to define health have been the result of the WHO definition. Parsons (1972) defines health in terms of the capacity to perform the socially assigned roles, while Sutherland and Fulton (1992) speak of "a reasonably optimistic and contented state of mind." While not the only definition, the WHO definition is widely cited because it can accommodate many others. For example, it accommodates Parsons (1972) because a state of complete social well-being would influence the capacity to perform socially assigned roles, and it considers Sutherland and Fulton's (1992) point because complete physical, mental, and social well-being would lead to a contented state of mind.

Regardless of how health is defined, unquestionably any activity, and therefore service, designed to improve health status must be classified as a health care service. Therefore, using the WHO definition, any service designed to improve the physical, mental, or social well-being of one individual or groups of individuals must be considered a health care service.

Medical care, while certainly one type of health care service, is not the entire health care system. Figure 1.1 shows the relationship of medical care to other health care services and health care, which is shown in relation to *health status*. In fact, an interesting study of the relationship of mortality to both medical care and to environmental variables revealed that the association of basic education with mortality rates in the United States was twice as strong as that of medical care expenditures and mortality (Auster, Leveson, and Sarachek 1969). Medical care must therefore be considered as only one, albeit an important one, of several types of services that can be correctly identified as health care services.

When referring to health care costs then, we should perhaps be more specific in identifying the particular component of health care; perhaps the true test lies in the evaluation of that component's positive contribution to health status, relative to the other components.

Medical Care and the Economic System

Like any other good or service, medical care is part of our economic system by virtue of the fact that it comprises services that are sold in the marketplace. In addition, medical care services, and all other health care services, play a unique role in the economic health of our country. As shown in Figure 1.1, medical care has the potential to affect health status in a positive manner. In this way, medical care is an input to health status. This is, of course, true of all other health care services. The effect on health status

Figure 1.1   Health Care and Medical Care in Perspective

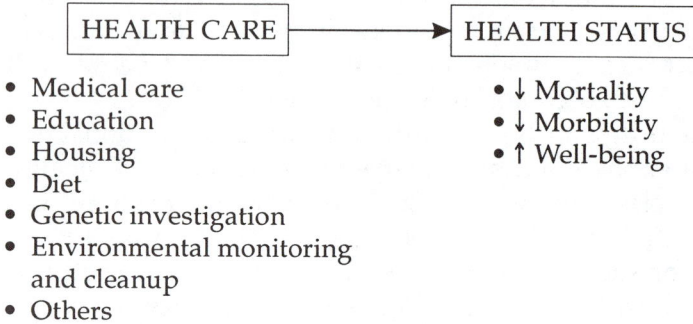

| HEALTH CARE | ⟶ | HEALTH STATUS |

- Medical care
- Education
- Housing
- Diet
- Genetic investigation
- Environmental monitoring and cleanup
- Others

- ↓ Mortality
- ↓ Morbidity
- ↑ Well-being

may manifest itself in a reduction of mortality or morbidity, or an increase in well-being.

To fully understand the economic implications of an improvement in health status, it is necessary to consider the human, or labor, contribution to the economic welfare of our society. This human contribution represents the necessary human resource in the production of any good or service. The contribution that any resource makes to any product is a function of the amount of the resource available for the production of the good or service and the relative ability of the resource to contribute to the production. In other words, production capability is affected by how much of the human resource is available and how productive that resource is.

Having operationally defined health status as some level of mortality, morbidity, and well-being, it is relatively simple to relate those measures to the population as we view it in terms of the human resource in the economic system. Since *mortality* is the loss of life, consider that it represents, economically speaking, a loss of all the person hours that would have been available to contribute to society's economic health had death been averted. A reduction in mortality translates into an increase in potential human resource hours (see Figure 1.2).

Morbidity is not so easy to define. It has been variously defined on a continuum that ranges from a comatose state to "not feeling well." A more widely accepted definition, however, would be one that includes the presence of some pathological condition

Figure 1.2   Effect of Health Status Measures on the Human
Resource

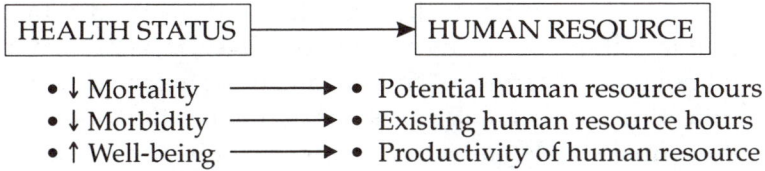

```
┌──────────────────┐          ┌────────────────────┐
│  HEALTH STATUS   │─────────▶│  HUMAN RESOURCE    │
└──────────────────┘          └────────────────────┘

  • ↓ Mortality    ──────▶  • Potential human resource hours
  • ↓ Morbidity    ──────▶  • Existing human resource hours
  • ↑ Well-being   ──────▶  • Productivity of human resource
```

or disease. For this discussion, this more specific definition, which
suggests a greater severity level than "not feeling well," will be
adopted. The presence of morbidity, as defined, would require
treatment that would at least interrupt normal activities of daily
living. Such treatment may not necessarily include a specific regimen of medical treatment, only a period of bed rest. As a result,
morbidity unambiguously leads to a reduction in the person hours
currently available for production. Reducing morbidity translates
into increasing current human resource hours (see Figure 1.2).

The final measure of health status under consideration is
well-being. This classification includes those who are "not feeling
well"—in general, those who are not sick enough to completely
absolve themselves of their regular daily activities, but also not
capable of attaining their usual level of performance. If a person
is incapable of attaining his or her usual level of performance, that
person is not as productive as he or she could be. A decline in well-
being, as defined here, results in the reduced productivity of the
individual. An increase in well-being translates into the increased
productivity of the human resource (see Figure 1.2).

It is now clear that medical care, or any other health care
service, has the potential to impact health status. It is also clear
that any change in health status represents a change in the human
resource. This means that, in terms of the economic system, the
human input has undergone a change. Given that the relative
productivity of any input represents a measure of the quality
of that input, a change in health status may manifest itself in a
change in the potential amount of the human resource available,
the existing amount of the human resource available, or the quality
of the human resource available.

Personal health and economic health

The economic health of society can be measured in many different ways. One of the most generally accepted and best indicators of the economic well-being of any society, however, is its annual total output of goods and services. This is sometimes referred to as the gross domestic product (GDP), which is defined as the total market value of all final goods and services produced in the economy in one year. As a measure of economic well-being, GDP has many shortcomings, and as a measure of the general welfare of society, it has many more shortcomings. It is not the purpose of this text to discuss the problems inherent in using GDP as a measure of economic health; many economics texts address that issue. For this discussion, GDP is an acceptable measure of the economic health of any society.

Economic health is, therefore, a function of many different inputs, one of which is the human input. A change in the amount or quality of any of these inputs will result in a change in economic health, as shown in Figure 1.3.

In suggesting the linkage between medical care and economic health, Figures 1.1, 1.2, and 1.3 demonstrate that medical care can influence health status, that health status represents a measure of the amount and quality of the human resource, and that the human resource is one of the inputs to economic health. To complete the

Figure 1.3   Effect of Human Resource on Economic Health

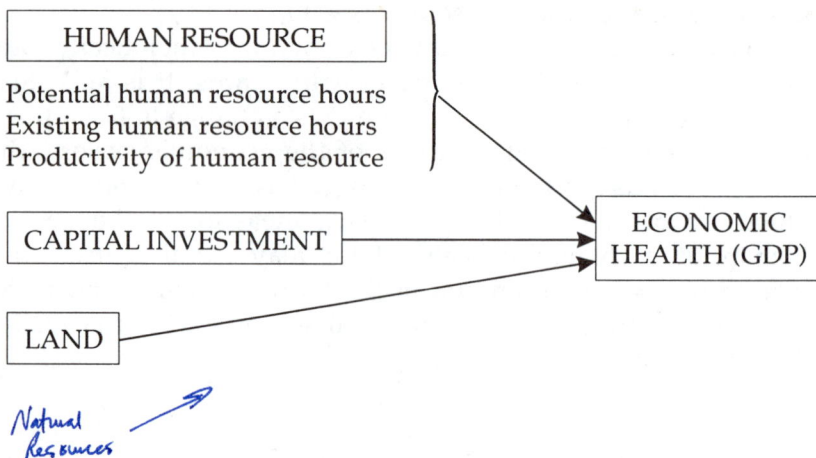

model scientifically—a model at best oversimplified and at worst inappropriate for a discussion of medical care—a final linkage is proposed. This connection represents the basis for the libertarian point of view, which holds that medical care services belong in the marketplace—that is, they are no different than any other good or service in the economy. The libertarian and egalitarian viewpoints, together with their potential influence on the medical care system, are explained in Chapter 2.

Economic health and use of medical care services

Expenditures on medical care generally increase as income increases. This is known as income elasticity, and simply means that the more money earned, the more spent on medical care services. Introductory economics texts teach that income, or perhaps more precisely disposable income, is a direct function of GDP—a measure sometimes referred to as income per capita that is derived by dividing by the number of people in the population.

Now, the basis for the libertarian argument can be clarified: It is argued that as the economy improves, income per capita increases, and consequently, more money is spent on medical care. As more money is spent on medical care, health status improves. Because human resources are increased in number or quality, more goods and services are produced, which translates into an increase in income per capita, which starts the process all over again. The fallacy of this argument, of course, is that there is no reason to expect that income is distributed in any way consistent with the need for medical care—that is, that any increase in expenditures on medical care will necessarily result from those experiencing income increases rather than from those experiencing greater need for medical care. Figure 1.4 exhibits the oversimplified, closed system model completed through this discussion.

Note that health status has become subsumed under *quantity* (potential and existing human resource hours) and *quality* (productivity of human resource) of the human resource. The interdependency of each component is illustrated, and it's clear that each component is both an input and an output. For example, medical care is an output of the economic health of society and an input to the quantity and quality (health status) of the human resource.

Figure 1.4   Medical Care, Health Care, and the Economic
System

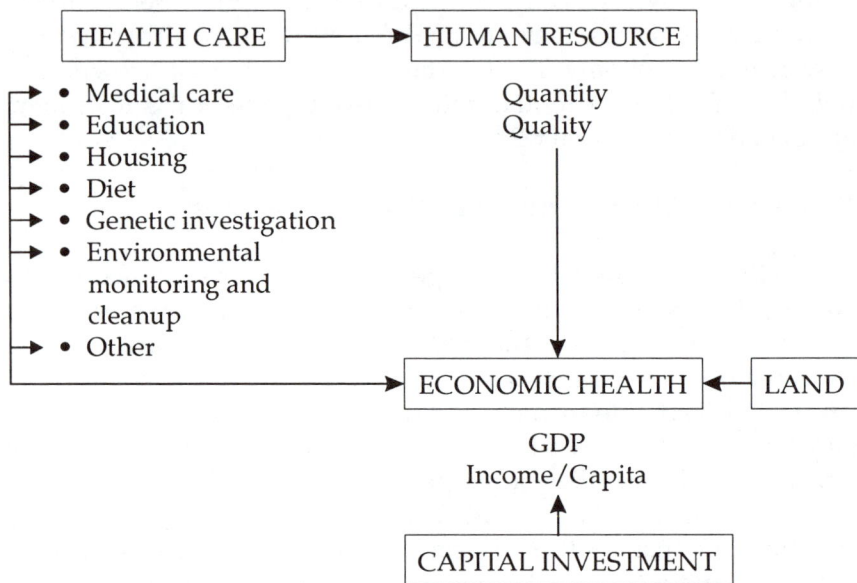

Input-Output Considerations of Medical Care

The input-output chain relationship between the components of
the economic system described in Figure 1.4 implies that each
component, or part of a component, can be viewed as either an
input or an output. This may not seem to be a particularly en-
lightening observation, but it is important because not only does
one's point of focus determine one's evaluation of the medical care
system, but the population's collective focus determines, to some
extent, the type of medical care system that will prevail. For this
discussion, *medical care system* refers to the organization, financing,
and delivery of medical care services.

The model has specified the influence of medical care on
health status; now that fact must be qualified. Medical care does
indeed have the "potential" to affect health status, but a possibility

is not a given. Some types of medical care services are more likely to have an effect on health status than others; they are more efficacious. It is also important to note that in providing a medical care service, it is possible for health status to be negatively affected. For example, when hospitalized, a patient is, in many cases, placed in an environment that poses a much greater threat of disease than the patient's normal environment. A patient's health status may also be negatively affected as the result of receiving a medical care service in error. For example, if the wrong drug is prescribed or prescriptions are inadvertently mixed, the patient can experience a decrease in well-being. Disease that is inadvertently induced by physicians or their treatment is known as iatrogenic disease.

Greater threat comes from an abnormally high number of virulent microorganisms, which include bacteria, fungi, and viruses, existing in all hospitals. The patient, in receiving one type of medical care service, can conceivably experience a decrease in well-being. This is known as a nosocomial infection. This type of condition is not necessarily the result of negligence or lack of caring, rather the combination of a debilitated patient in an environment that houses many other sick people. It is an unavoidable aspect of medical care that many patients share the same facilities and equipment while undergoing diagnosis and treatment.

Both nosocomial infections and iatrogenic disease are troublesome features of the medical care system, but considerable effort is expended on the monitoring and containment of such conditions. A constant awareness and continued vigilance of these phenomena in the medical care system keeps them in the proper perspective— as a concern but not a crisis. Nevertheless, nosocomial infection and iatrogenic disease are illustrative of how providing a medical care service can negatively affect health status.

From an economic perspective, there is another concern regarding the relationship between medical care services and health status that approaches crisis proportions. This concern is that of providing a service that impacts health status neither positively or negatively. Individually, everyone would surely agree that it is less of a crisis to have no impact than to have a negative impact on health status. Societywide, however, the potential damage that results from providing medical care services that have no impact on health status is enormous. Whereas only certain types of service are likely to have a negative effect on health status, all services can conceivably have zero effect on health status.

This postulate is better understood by borrowing from the field of economics. Economic theory provides us with the concepts of *marginal benefit* and *marginal cost*. Simply put, this means for a given additional expenditure (cost), how much do we get (benefit)? To bring these concepts into the context of this discussion, For a given additional medical service (cost), how much improvement in health status do we receive (benefit)? The economic consequences of providing a service that has no effect on health status can now be appreciated: there is a cost but no benefit. The magnitude of such consequences is potentially limitless. To recognize this, the concept of marginal benefit (improvement in health status) must be explored further.

It is, of course, possible that the very first medical care service provided to any individual will have no effect on that individual's health status. It may be an ineffective service for the suspected pathological condition, or there may, in fact, be no pathological condition. In either case, the health status of the individual does not change as a result of receiving the service. A more likely case, however, is that of a sick patient and an available service(s) that potentially can influence health status. To simplify, consider a patient who has a strep throat where the service available is a penicillin shot. The first service (penicillin shot) will probably contribute positively and significantly to the patient's health status. The second penicillin shot may also contribute positively and significantly to the patient's health status. A point will be reached, however, where an additional shot may contribute positively to the patient's health status, but the additional contribution will be less than the previous incremental improvement. This declining incremental improvement in health status will continue until another critical point is reached. It is that point at which an additional service (penicillin shot) will not have any positive impact on health status. Note that the cost to provide each subsequent penicillin shot is the same although the benefit derived from subsequent penicillin shots decreases.

A generalization regarding medical care service and health status can be derived from this example. Although there may be a positive relationship between the provision of medical care service and health status, it is not necessarily a linear one. That is, it is not necessarily a fixed-ratio relationship that continues over any number of services provided (see Figure 1.5a), but rather a curvilinear relationship or changing-ratio relationship (see Figure 1.5b).

Figure 1.5 provides a simple but graphic presentation of an important phenomenon: the contribution to health status provided by any medical care service is a function of present health status and of how many services have previously been provided. Further, for any and all services, there will be a particular point where additional services will contribute nothing to health status. This phenomenon is consistent with Enthoven's postulate, "flat of the curve medicine" (Enthoven 1980) (which is cited in many works but discussed particularly well in Evans' excellent 1984 book on the economics of Canadian health care and in Pauly's 1988 work describing competition in medical care). Iatrogenic disease and nosocomial infections would show up in Figure 1.5b as a downturn in the line depicting the relationship between health status and number of services (Illich 1976).

At this point, a reader may ask why medical care services that have no impact on health status are provided. Certainly, it could be argued from an economic, or efficiency, perspective that no service

Figure 1.5   Relationship of Medical Care Services to Health Status: (a) linear, (b) curvilinear

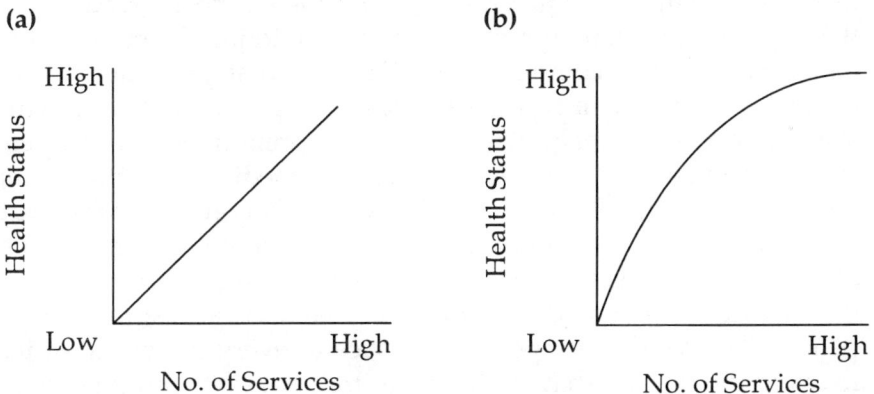

(a)

(b)

should be provided that does not contribute positively to health status. However, forces are present that violate this argument. For example, in situations where total reimbursement is a function of the number of transactions that take place, more transactions will occur. A good example of this can be found in an industry where a piecework method of reimbursement is sometimes adopted. The more "pieces" the operator produces, the greater the reimbursement. Since medical care providers are often reimbursed on a per-transaction basis, there is an incentive to provide more services in order to increase reimbursement. This does not necessarily imply that the provision of additional services does not contribute positively to health status, rather that the motive for doing so is based on reimbursement and not health status considerations. This phenomenon is known as the *marginal revenue effect.* Regardless of the motive for providing additional services, the principle of the declining positive contribution to health status discussed above applies to all services. Conceivably, a point will be reached with any service where additional services will not contribute positively to health status. It is also conceivable that the motive for providing additional services is provided by the marginal revenue effect. The incentive is present to some extent when medical care facilities are reimbursed on a cost basis.

Another motive for providing services beyond the point where they have no positive effect on health status can be found in the interface of our medical and legal systems. Evidence exists linking the incidence of malpractice suits to the magnitude of individual awards. It could be argued that the concomitant increase in malpractice insurance premiums has been greater than the experience with malpractice awards would justify, but it is this barometer of the malpractice environment that promotes action on the part of the medical care services provider. Faced with sharply increasing malpractice insurance premiums and the persuasive powers of the insurance industry, medical care providers are convinced that the threat of a lawsuit is, not only very real, but ever-present. The legal profession must also shoulder some of the blame for this sensitive malpractice climate. Rightly or wrongly, the medical care provider, under these circumstances, feels compelled to provide every possible service to every patient in order to avoid the lawsuit that would claim that not everything possible was done for the patient. This is known as practicing defensive medicine, and it could lead to providing medical care services that do not contribute positively to health status.

Another more prevalent and more noble motive for providing services beyond the point where they have no positive impact on health status is in the genuine desire on the part of the provider to do everything possible for the patient. It could be suggested that this motivation is not attenuated as more and more services are provided. Perhaps, the desire to provide more services is not assuaged even when the point is reached where additional services will not contribute positively to health status.

Finally on this subject, increasing patient demand may persuade a physician to provide a service or procedure that cannot possibly have a positive effect on health status. However, by providing a service or procedure demanded by a patient, patient expectations can be met and anxiety reduced. A good example is in prescribing antibiotics to treat viral infections. This is not to argue that in every case it is better to knowingly provide a service that cannot possibly impact health status, rather to suggest that in some cases it may be appropriate.

Structure, Process, and Outcome

A somewhat similar motivating force emanates from the general understanding of the very relationship between medical care services and health status that is being discussed here. In an attempt to better understand this phenomenon, we now draw on some of the work of one of the leading scholars in this field, Avedis Donabedian (1980, 1982, 1985).

As previously suggested, providing a medical care service that did not contribute positively to health status is unacceptable from an economic perspective. It is also unacceptable from a medical standpoint. Surely very few would disagree with the suggestion that if the medical care system exists to meet a need, that need must certainly be the need to maximize the health status of the population. Given that maximum health status for the total population is perhaps more of a highly desirable abstract notion than an attainable reality, it is reasonable to suggest that our population is never in that state. It then follows that the health status of the population is always such that a positive contribution to health status is always possible. The contribution that the medical care system or an individual medical care service make to the health status of the population or an individual is recognized as the *outcome* of the system or service.

There is little dispute among scholars who have followed Donabedian that the medical care system should rightfully be evaluated and judged by its outcomes. This may appear to be a rather obvious conclusion, but having agreed that outcomes should be evaluated, the scholarly community becomes divided on the issue of how outcomes should be operationalized and measured. This division is not of an arbitrary nature and certainly not one resulting from widely disparate philosophical positions. It emanates from the paradoxical position in which the scholars find themselves. The more inclusive their definition of health and therefore health status, the more difficult it is to measure. To think of measuring health status or a change in health status with an operational definition of health that reflected the WHO definition of good health is mind-boggling. And although scholars disagree as what to include in the definition and measurement of outcomes, most agree on the difficulty of the task.

Given the components of health status adopted herein—mortality, morbidity, and well-being—readers may, at this point, appreciate the difficulty discussed above. To accept mortality rates only as a measure of health status would make measuring outcomes reasonably simple. The problem is, however, at the population level where mortality is not very sensitive to the intervention of medical care. In other words, how much medical care would it take to engender a measurable change in the mortality rates? At the other extreme, if one insists that mortality, morbidity, and well-being are included in the measure of health status, the task of measuring outcomes becomes almost impossible.

Can this dilemma be resolved? Donabedian's work describes how others have responded to this challenge (Donabedian 1980, 1982, 1985).

Medical care services do not appear magically; they are the result of a process similar to that used in the production of any other good or service. Facilities in which the services are produced are required, and human and nonhuman resources must be employed—all of which function in a production process. In this case, it is the process of producing medical care services. If all of the facilities and human and nonhuman resources are included under the rubric of inputs, then, consistent with the earlier discussion of resources, the type or quality of these inputs can be determined. For example, all hospitals are not the same, all physicians do not receive the same training, and all other hospital personnel are not equally well-trained or competent.

Intuitively, we know that the variation in the quality of the inputs results in a variation in the quality of the outcomes. Donabedian (1980) refers to these inputs as the *structure* of medical care. The relationship between structure and outcome might therefore be described as "good structure increases the likelihood of leading to good outcome." Good structure in this context connotes some level of excellence in the facility, the training and competence of the physicians and other personnel, and the capital equipment. The higher the level of these inputs, the greater is the potential for a positive impact on health status.

But it is possible to employ the best possible resources and combine them in a manner that results in less than the best possible results. The inputs may be first-rate, but the production process is poor. The production *process* might be described as the steps that take place toward producing a good or service. For example, in the old-fashioned, full-service gas station, the process might be oversimplified as follows: the car arrives at the pump; the attendant walks to the car and determines the service required (e.g., a fill-up); the attendant performs the service (e.g., fills the tank with gas); and the driver pays the stipulated amount for the service. Analogously, the process of production of medical care is that which takes place while patients are being treated. Unfortunately, patients are usually not in the same, and enviable, position of the car driver at the gas station because they do not know exactly what they want. Nevertheless, the steps that take place during diagnosis and treatment are recognized by scholars as the "process" of medical care (Donabedian 1980).

Therefore, despite a good structure, poor process may indeed lead to poor outcome. Yet, good structure and good process have the potential to contribute to good outcome. In other words, excellent facilities, excellently trained and competent personnel, and an excellent process improve significantly the chances of making a positive contribution to health status. Note, this statement does not *guarantee* that good outcomes necessarily result from good structure and good process, but it does make that event more likely. Figure 1.6 illustrates this concept; a more complete discussion will come later.

We can now return to those forces that motivate the provision of medical care services beyond the point where they have no effect on health status. Again, it is extremely difficult to measure all but the grossest operational definition of health status. It is much easier instead to measure levels of excellence of the structural components and the activities included in the process. For example, hospital size, physician specialty, number of inpatient days, and number of laboratory tests can all be easily measured. The results of many scholarly investigations have shown that generally there is a strong relationship between structure, process, and outcome. For example, Riedel and Riedel (1979) found that specialists consistently complied with more explicit criteria of good care than generalists in the treatment of hypertension, chest pain, abdominal pain, urinary tract infection, and pharyngitis. Payne et al. (1976) found that size of hospital and modal specialty (specialty appropriate for the particular case) had a positive effect on admissions and length of stay. Rhee (1975) found that board certification

Figure 1.6   The Relationship of Structure, Process, and Outcome

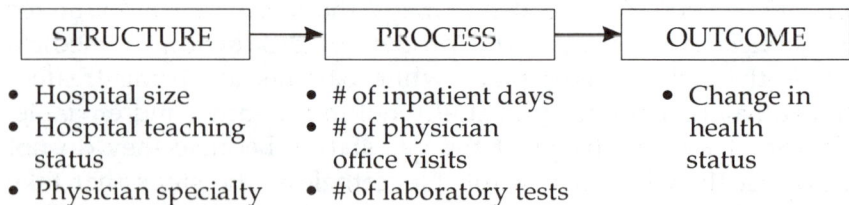

STRUCTURE	→	PROCESS	→	OUTCOME
• Hospital size • Hospital teaching status • Physician specialty		• # of inpatient days • # of physician office visits • # of laboratory tests		• Change in health status

Note: Adapted and reprinted from *Explorations in Quality Assessment and Monitoring. Vol. I: The Definition of Quality and Approaches to Its Assessment* by Avedis Donabedian, published by Health Administration Press. © 1980. See also Avedis Donabedian, "Evaluating the Quality of Medical Care," *Milbank Memorial Fund Quarterly* 44 (1966): 166–203.

and board certification with subspecialty had a positive effect on physician performance scores in the episode of care for 15 diagnoses. He found further that hospitals with a higher level of formal organization had higher physician performance scores. Interestingly too, Rhee found that less highly trained physicians in highly organized facilities had better performance scores than highly trained physicians in less highly organized facilities. Although volume of procedures may not be seen as a measure of facility size, it certainly is indicative of facility capability. Luft et al. (1990) provide evidence of the relationship between volume and patient outcome. This work is discussed further in Chapter 8.

As a result, imputing a measure of outcome from the measures of structure and/or process is possible. In other words, we can accept the fact that good structure and/or good process result in good outcomes and, consequently, are satisfied to concentrate on the improvement of structure and process. To the extent that we are aware of what attributes of structure contribute to good process and what attributes of good process contribute to good outcomes this is a reasonable assumption. A problem arises when "good process" is misinterpreted or misapplied.

The concept of the marginal benefit associated with additional medical care services is not always understood by those who provide or arrange for care. In particular, they are unaware of the possibility that progressively smaller positive contributions to health status may result from providing an increasing number of services. It may be perceived that if providing a particular service has a positive effect on health status, providing an additional service will have a similar incremental beneficial effect, or colloquially, "If one is good, more must be better."

This misunderstanding can result in providing services beyond the point where they make no positive contribution to health status. It also leads to a confusion of the input-output relationship existing between process and outcome: This discussion has demonstrated that medical care services are an input to health status (output), and when this relationship is ignored or misunderstood, the focus of attention falls on the medical care service (input). The service in and of itself then becomes the only important consideration, and the "more is better" attitude prevails. Under these circumstances, the input (medical care services) has been ascribed the role of an output. The true reason for providing medical care services (the improvement of health status) is lost in the impetus to increase what is now erroneously considered output (services). The reports from almost any medical care service–providing organization document how greatly organization objectives are influenced by this kind of thinking where improving health status becomes submerged.

Health Status and Economic Health

Our model shows that just as medical care services are an input to health status, health status is an input to economic health. Again, this is important because health status can be considered an output or an input. We have seen how the different input-output perspectives can result in very different approaches to the provision of medical care services; the same is true of the perspective of health status. If health status is considered an output, which is the objective of the medical care system, the resulting medical care system will differ from one that results from an approach that considers health status an input to economic health. (Remember that in this text, the medical care system includes the organization, financing, and delivery of medical care services.) If health status, or improvement in health status, is recognized as the appropriate output of the medical care system, then the maximum improvement in, or the highest level of, health status for the entire population is the ultimate goal. This concept implies that every individual in the population is equally important, and that improving the health status of a 65-year-old person is just as beneficial to our society as improving that of a 25-year-old person.

On the other hand, if health status or improved health status is viewed strictly as an input to the economic health of a society rather than a desirable goal in and of itself, the resulting medical care system will reflect this perspective. It is inevitable when this view of health status is taken that any emphasis placed on improving health status will be confined to those who are currently providing the human resources for the economic system and those who have the potential to contribute to the economic system. Those who no longer have the potential to contribute to the economic system will be ignored. So, when this perspective of health status prevails, the value of good health is greater for a 25-year-old person than for a 65-year-old person, or on a more basic level, that the life of a 25-year-old is worth more than the life of a 65-year-old. (Chapter 2 will provide a detailed presentation of the influence social values have on the medical care system, but for this discussion it is sufficient to point out that the medical care system will reflect this value.)

In this thinking, services designed to address the disease conditions of younger people will predominate and those designed to address the disease conditions of the elderly will be of low priority. In addition, the financing mechanism will be designed to minimize the financial barrier to access for the younger people while the elderly receive no such relief. Interestingly enough, Great Britain once had a system such as this. During the period 1911–1948, a compulsory national health insurance program that was the forerunner of the British National Health Service was in place (Curran 1970). This insurance program, however, covered only those persons directly employed for wages; the unemployed dependents of these workforce members were not covered under any circumstances. At that time, Britain apparently believed that health status was important in its contribution to economic health. By 1948, Great Britain changed its health plan's emphasis, giving birth to the National Health Service, which would cover all of the population regardless of employment status (Eckstein 1958).

Many scholars have suggested that the level of industrial development is highly correlated with the perspective from which health status is viewed: countries that are emerging as industrialized powers are more likely to view health status as an input to economic growth while their more industrially developed counterparts view health status as an output. Swartz (1993) argues, for example, that employers who had problems recruiting and maintaining a labor force in Canada in the early 1930s saw health insurance as a way to increase labor efficiency. And King (1973) recognized the benefit of health insurance in most industrialized countries as contributing to the industry of individuals.

There is perhaps a disappointing subscript to this theory. It is apparently possible to evolve economically without subscribing entirely to the view of health status as an output and to reach a stage of development where medical care services are viewed as an output. As discussed earlier, this is "flat of the curve" medical care—the point at which services provided, regardless of the impact on health status, are considered to be desirable.

The next chapter will provide a much more detailed discussion of the effect that societal values have on the form that our medical care system takes.

Discussion Questions

1. If medical care is not synonymous with health care, what are the implications for resource allocation to the medical care sector?

2. What issues should we be concerned with regarding the allocation of medical care services given the suggested relationship between personal health and economic health?

3. What are the major contributors to and the implications of "flat of curve" medical care?

4. What difference would we expect to see in a medical care system that considered medical care as output, as opposed to in a medical care system that considered it an input?

References

Auster, R., I. Leveson, and D. Sarachek. "The Production of Health, An Exploratory Study." *The Journal of Human Resources* 4 (1969): 411–36.

Curran, W. J. "Nationalized Health Services: The British Experience." In *Health Services Administration: Policy Cases and the Case Method*, edited by R. Penchansky. Cambridge, MA: Harvard University Press, 1970.

Donabedian, A. *Explorations in Quality Assessment and Monitoring. Vol. 2: The Criteria and Standards of Quality.* Ann Arbor, MI: Health Administration Press, 1982.

———. *Explorations in Quality Assessment and Monitoring. Vol. 1: The Definition of Quality and Approaches to Its Assessment.* Ann Arbor, MI: Health Administration Press, 1980.

———. *Explorations in Quality Assessment and Monitoring. Vol. 3: The Methods and Findings of Quality Assessment and Monitoring.* Ann Arbor, MI: Health Administration Press, 1985.

Eckstein, H. *The English Health Service: Its Origins, Structure and Achievements.* Cambridge, MA: Harvard University Press, 1958.

Enthoven, A. S. *Health Plan: The Only Practical Solution to the Soaring Costs of Medical Care.* Reading, MA: Addison-Wesley, 1980.

Evans, R. G. *Strained Mercy: The Economics of Canadian Health Care.* Toronto, Ontario: Butterworths, 1984.

Illich, I. *Medical Nemesis.* New York: Pantheon Books, 1976.

King, W. L. M. *Industry and Humanity.* Toronto, Ontario: University of Toronto Press, 1973.

Luft, H. S., D. W. Garnick, D. H. Mark, and S. J. McPhee. *Hospital Volume, Physician Volume, and Patient Outcomes.* Ann Arbor, MI: Health Administration Press, 1990.

Parsons, T. "Definitions of Health and Illness in Light of American Values and Social Structure." In *Patients, Physicians and Illness,* 2d ed., edited by E. G. Jaco. New York: Free Press, 1972.

Pauly, M. V. "A Primer on Competition in Medical Markets". In *Health Care in America,* edited by E. H. Frech III. San Francisco: Pacific Research Institute for Public Policy, 1988.

Payne, B. C., T. F. Lyons, L. Dworshius, M. Kolton, and W. Morris. *The Quality of Medical Care: Evaluation and Improvement.* Chicago: The Hospital Education and Research Trust, 1976.

Rhee, S. *Relative Influences of Specialty Status, Organization of Office Care and Organization of Hospital Care on the Quality of Medical Care: A Multivariate Analysis.* Ph.D. diss., University of Michigan, Ann Arbor, 1975.

Riedel, R. L., and D. E. Riedel. *Practice and Performance: An Assessment of Ambulatory Care.* Ann Arbor, MI: Health Administration Press, 1979.

Somers, A. R., and H. M. Somers. *Health and Health Care.* Germantown, MD: Aspen Systems, 1977.

Sutherland, R. W., and M. J. Fulton. *Health Care in Canada,* 3d ed. Ottawa, Canada: The Health Group. Distributed by The Canadian Public Health Association, Ottawa, Canada, 1992.

Swartz, D. "The Politics of Reform: Public Health Insurance in Canada." *Internationl Journal of Health Services* 23 (1993): 219–38.

World Health Organization. "Constitution." In *The First Ten Years of the World Health Organization.* Geneva, Switzerland: The World Health Organization, 1958.

Chapter 2

Social Values and the Medical Care System

This chapter suggests that there is a continuum of social values, with the egalitarian value set at one end and the libertarian value set at the other. The values most relevant to medical care—freedom, equality, rewards, and treatment of the poor—can be identified as lying somewhere on the continuum (Donabedian 1971, 1973). Four components of the U.S. and Canadian medical care systems are then examined, and the relative position on the social values continuum is discussed for each component in each system.

In Chapter 1, the libertarian argument was clear in studying the closed system model. In that context, the libertarian argument might have been summed up in the statement, "Let the market take care of it." The "it," of course, is the distribution of medical care services.

However, a medical care system will more likely reflect political as opposed to economic decisions. Theoretically, the decision-makers (politicians) in a democratic system represent the values of their constituents, and as a result, the social values of the majority become reflected in the policy decisions. A discussion as to how well politicians represent the values of their constituents is beyond the scope of this book, but it is reasonable to assume that in a democratic system the social values of the population are reflected by its political representatives and policy decisions reflect the social values of its people. The libertarian viewpoint represents one set of social values among several possible sets.

Regardless of labels, social values influence the shape and the function of all societal institutions, and the institutionalized delivery of medical care is no exception. This may appear somewhat obvious, but it is extremely important to recognize that one should not expect to find similar medical care systems in societies that have different value systems. For example, many have been tempted into making cross-national comparisons between Canada and the United States without seriously considering the different social values in the two nations. The social values in the United States make it difficult to conceive of adoption of the single-source reimbursement system, yet it is one of the most often cited reasons for the apparent greater efficiency in the Canadian system.

At the risk of contributing to previous misinterpretations of these two value sets, let us recognize the types of policy decisions that emerge when the policymakers are of different political parties. For example, medical care policies in the United States have traditionally been quite different when the Democratic Party (ideologically more egalitarian) controls the executive and/or legislative branches than when the Republican Party (ideologically more libertarian) does. Likewise in Canada, the Progressive Conservatives (ideologically more libertarian) enact quite different medical care policies than does the National Democratic Party (ideologically more egalitarian).

While few societies may fit the libertarian or egalitarian ideals any society can be placed at some point on the continuum, closer to one end than the other. Different components of any system within the same society may be more or less influenced by the values of that society. In the same society, for example, the various components of the medical care system may appear at variant points on the value set continuum.

How do the positions of these two value systems affect the medical care system? We will explore this question by identifying the major contributing value system by the character of its medical care system components.

Libertarian values

At the core of the libertarian philosophy is the notion that individuals are responsible for their own achievements. Libertarians would be likely to argue that nothing unearned should be given to individuals because it would be both morally and economically injurious. The closed system discussed in Chapter 1 would satisfy the libertarians in that it would be viewed as rewarding individuals according to the value of their contribution to the economic system. In other words, those that contribute to the economic system receive the wherewithal to purchase the goods and services produced by the system. Medical care services, the libertarians would argue, are no different from any other service and are therefore rightfully part of the reward system.

In the tradition of Adam Smith, the libertarian philosophy would subscribe to the notion that with individuals pursuing their own best personal interest, the interest of society as a whole is best served[1] (Ferguson and Maurice 1970). However, recognizing that most disease is involuntary and that all economic nonachievers are not necessarily "guilty of malingering," the libertarians would accept the fact that there are what they might term the "worthy poor." Charity would take care of the "worthy poor" because libertarians believe that charity not only benefits the recipient, it ennobles the giver. The offer of charity would not, of course, extend to the malingerers; the libertarians would expect that any recipient of this largesse would be first encouraged to muster all personal and family resources. The amount of charity dispensed would be such that the recipients would not be as financially established as individuals who were self-supporting.

For those who are sick because they voluntarily engaged in disease-causing behavior, libertarians would argue that they do not qualify for assistance. They believe, for example, that smokers should pay higher health insurance premiums than nonsmokers.

Milton Friedman (1962), one of the preeminent libertarians of modern America, reminds us that "in the late eighteenth and early nineteenth centuries the intellectual movement that went under the name of liberalism emphasized freedom as the ultimate goal of society." This freedom is still at the heart of the libertarian philosophy, as is opposition to any government intervention, except when the protection of freedom represents an encroachment on freedom. Friedman (1962) also points out that the term *liberal* has since been "corrupted" to now be used to describe those with completely polar philosophies—that is, the egalitarians. Libertarians define equality in terms of constitutional and legal equality, not equal rewards. It is from this legally defined framework that competition among equals emanates.

Egalitarian values

Egalitarians would argue that economic failure should not be equated with moral failure, and therefore, rewards should not be tied to economic success. Good health—and therefore medical care—is a prerequisite for economic success and as such should not be part of the reward system. In other words, medical care does not belong in the marketplace. They would also argue that medical care services are so unique that they do not readily lend themselves to market forces.

Medical care and the marketplace

Before discussing the egalitarian value system more comprehensively, let us briefly consider some of these market forces relative to the characteristics of medical care services. A market system requires that there be rational consumers, but consumers of medical care services (clients) cannot act in a rational manner for several reasons. In most cases, clients are not aware of their true need for medical care. Very rarely is there 100 percent agreement (*congruence*) between physician and client as to what constitutes the need for medical care (Donabedian 1973). (Congruence is discussed in detail in Chapter 9.)

In addition, there is no way for clients to determine from where the "best" care might be obtained. They are not aware of all possible alternatives, and they do not purchase care often enough to develop this knowledge. For example, through a process of repeated usage that might include seeing several providers, clients can form opinions regarding their perception of the best barber, without ever being convinced that all barbers are of the same quality. However, a great deal of effort is expended by the medical profession to convince clients that all physicians are of a like quality. While to some, this may seem necessary in order to inspire the client's confidence in the physician, it does inhibit the client from searching for the "best": there is no "best" among equals.

It is perhaps a revealing comment on this issue to note that relicensure of a physician is not tied to reexamination. The notion that physicians who graduated 30 years ago are of the same quality as those who graduated three years ago requires the leap of faith that all physicians remained current through continuing education.

Remember also that until very recently, the medical profession would not allow advertising of any kind. While it could be argued that some advertising is unethical, it certainly is not true that all advertising is unethical. In fact, advertising can be a most effective way of educating the consumer, providing it is done responsibly. Paul Feldstein (1988) discusses this issue in detail and argues effectively that advertising leads to lower, rather than higher, prices.

Consequently, although it is not possible for clients to become as completely informed regarding the use of medical care services as they might be about the use of a barber's services, to suggest that a conspiracy exists to keep the client uninformed may not be so outlandish. However, this barrier is beginning to crumble as clients become more willing to question the physician's process of care and potential for a desirable outcome.

Clients also may not act rationally because the consumption of medical care services may be unpleasant. The very act of being treated (consuming a medical care service) can be a physically unpleasant experience, and therefore, clients may be reluctant to seek out the service even when they are certain they need it. This makes medical care consumption unlike any normal service in the marketplace where the client dictates demand. Generally, the client makes a decision to buy based on the perceived benefit from consuming the service, the price of the service, and the client's income. Very often the need for medical care is unpredictable, unwanted, and urgent. Even when this is not so, those who demand the majority of medical care services are the physicians (the providers) themselves. Once the client has made the initial contact with the provider, the provider makes decisions about all additional services, not the consumer. For example, who among us, if told by a physician that we should be hospitalized or that we should come back next week, would decline?

Another possible reason for not including medical services in the marketplace is that supply is not the result of demand. Under true market conditions, supply is a lagged response to the demand, so that when the quantity demanded increases (or decreases), existing (or potential) suppliers move to expand (or decrease) their supply. It is strictly a rational reaction to the activity in the market (Ferguson and Maurice 1970).

While it is important to the egalitarian value system that medical care not be part of the market system, other points are equally important. The egalitarian viewpoint would also stress the fact that charity can be demeaning, particularly when it identifies and sets apart the recipient. To avoid the evolution of a two-tier system of medical care—one for the poor and one for the nonpoor—egalitarians would argue that poor clients (so-called charity cases) should be mainstreamed, which could be achieved by ensuring that everyone, regardless of ability to pay, has access to the system without special identifying access credentials. This could mean anything from determining that health care is a right and that all citizens are entitled to access without any proof of eligibility, to the provision of health insurance for all citizens with identical proof of eligibility.

The egalitarian concept of freedom is derived from the principle that freedom is the presence of real opportunity to make choices from a set of alternatives. Imbedded in this concept is the notion that total freedom comprises a set of many individual freedoms and that the concern should be with the totality of freedoms rather than freedom in reference to every issue that might face an individual. For example, by taking away one freedom through imposing compulsory, universal health insurance, individuals become free from the fear of having to pay a large medical bill and have the freedom to seek care at any time. Similarly, by taking away one freedom through imposing compulsory retirement insurance, individuals become free from the fear of how they will survive financially as they age.

This egalitarian concept of freedom might explain the use of isolation hospitals for patients with tuberculosis or other infectious diseases in the early part of this century.

Table 2.1 summarizes the philosophies of the two value sets.

Table 2.1 Summary of Egalitarian and Libertarian Values

	Egalitarian	*Libertarian*
Freedom	Restriction of one freedom can enhance another, with the result that total freedoms are increased.	Freedom from government interference except to protect freedom. Individual is responsible for own achievements.
Equality	Equal rewards.	Equal opportunity, constitutionally and legally.
The poor	Poor clients should be mainstreamed. Charity is demeaning.	The worthy poor should receive charity. Benefits should be less than those who work. All personal wealth should be mustered first.
Medical care	Prerequisite to good health. Successful participation in economic system dependent on good health—therefore on medical care. It does not belong in the marketplace.	Part of the reward system. Economic success allows purchase of medical care. It belongs in the marketplace.

Note: This draws on the work of Avedis Donabedian, *Aspects of Medical Care Administration: Specifying Requirements for Health Care*, Cambridge, MA: Harvard University Press for the Commonwealth Fund, 1973.

Impact of Social Value on Medical Care Systems

At the beginning of this chapter, it was suggested that social values shape all social organizations and that the medical care system, as one social organization, is no exception. We will now briefly consider the components of a medical care system relative to the social values discussed above. While the medical care system comprises several different activities and each one is subject to the influence of social values, each one will not necessarily be influenced to the same degree. For this discussion, the following activities of the medical care system are identified: method of financing the system, mode of delivery of care, method of provider reimbursement, and resource allocation.

Method of financing the system

In a society with strong libertarian values, we would expect to find a medical care system that was financed entirely by individuals paying for the care they received in the marketplace. The existence of voluntary private health insurance would not violate the libertarian value set because clients would be free to purchase health insurance coverage at various levels of comprehensivity in the market for health insurance. In this environment, the private health insurers then become the major source of funding for the medical care system.

In a society with strong egalitarian values, we would expect to find a medical care system financed by some level of government through general revenues or a special fund that derives from compulsory and universal health insurance. The governmental body, as legitimate representatives of the people, would be the major source of funding for the medical care system.

Mode of delivery

Under libertarian influences we would expect to find a medical care system that relied heavily on the individual entrepreneur provider and on private, investor-owned facilities. Each one of these would compete for clients in providing services that reflected the needs of those clients able to pay for them, either out of pocket or through health insurance. Solo or small-group private practice would be the predominant mode of delivery of physician care, and investor-owned (for-profit) hospitals of the size that took advantage of economies of scale would be the rule. There would be little or no attempt to organize the system into a whole.

In contrast, in an egalitarian society we would expect to find physicians practicing in large multispecialty clinics and inpatient care delivered by variably sized government-owned hospitals in a completely organized system. These providers and facilities would provide services that reflected the needs of the total population in which they were located because the entire population would be eligible to receive care.

Method of provider reimbursement

Regardless of the manner in which the system is financed, the method of reimbursing providers and facilities is a separate consideration. Under libertarian influences, physicians would be reimbursed on a fee-for-service basis with fees being determined by the physicians in response to forces in the marketplace. Hospitals would be reimbursed on a price per unit of output. That unit could be any one of several that might be appropriate for a multiproduct firm—for example, per diem or per case.

In an egalitarian society, on the other hand, physicians would be salaried employees of the government, and hospitals would be government-owned and financed through a yearly budget.

Resource allocation

In a completely libertarian society, the number and type of physicians produced by the educational system would be determined entirely by the desires of would-be physicians and their assessment of the chances for success. The location of physicians would also be determined entirely by the physicians, without necessarily taking into account the needs of the population. In other words, if a physician of a particular specialty felt that he or she could be successful in a given area, regardless of the number of physicians already present and regardless of the need in the population, he or she would be at liberty to practice there.

A libertarian influence would also dictate that a hospital could locate anywhere it thought it could be financially viable. In competing for clients, each hospital would employ, to the extent possible, the latest technology without regard for duplication of services and resources in serving the same population.

In contrast, in an egalitarian society, we would expect to find the number, type, and location of physicians to be much more consistent with the need in the population. This would be determined by the government and effected with the use of incentives and controls. The number and location of hospitals, together with the technology employed, would also be orchestrated through the use of controls and incentives applied by the government. There would be very little duplication of resources or facilities with the government attempting to achieve a distribution of medical care service–producing units that was more consistent with the need for care than with the wealth of the population.

Examining two systems and their values: The United States and Canada

A purely libertarian or purely egalitarian system probably does not exist. Most systems are a mix with the dominance of one or the other orientation. At the risk of oversimplifying the above discussion, we can consider the U.S. and Canadian medical care systems relative to the above four components and determine which value sets predominated.

Method of financing and mode of delivery

In the U.S. system, the predominant mode of physician practice is solo or small-group practice, with physicians generally functioning as entrepreneurs. Although some form of managed care exists, the impetus for such arrangements generally emanates from the desire to control costs. There is very little effort to organize the total system, and very little government involvement in the delivery of care. The exception to this is the Veterans Affairs (VA) system where the hospitals are government-owned and the physicians are government employees. Overall, U.S. hospitals are in the private sector; approximately 12 percent are investor-owned, 57 percent are nongovernment, not-for-profit, and 31 percent are government-owned (American Hospital Association 1993). The climate in the United States centers on private-sector activity, reflecting strong libertarian values. Note that even in the one area that the government is involved, the VA, it could be characterized as part of a reward system—reward for having served one's country.

In the Canadian system, the predominant physician practice mode is also solo or small-group practice. Since all people are eligible for all levels of care, there is a greater effort to coordinate these levels of care, but there is no total system organization. Physicians are private entrepreneurs, and hospitals generally are not government-owned. In fact, approximately 5 percent of the hospitals in Canada are investor-owned, with 48 percent nongovernment, not-for-profit, and 47 percent government-owned (Canadian Hospital Association 1993).

There is slightly more government involvement in the delivery of care in Canada and less emphasis in the hospital sector on for-profit facilities, so for this component of the system, Canada is only marginally more egalitarian than the United States.

Method of provider reimbursement

The system in the United States is financed through a mixture of private and public funding. In 1991, the federal Medicare program accounted for 18 percent of total health care expenditures and is funded through a compulsory payroll deduction, general revenue, and premiums. The federal-state Medicaid program accounts for 14 percent of total health care expenditures and is funded predominantly through general revenue. The public sector finances 44 percent of total health care expenditures, the private sector, 56 percent (Burner, Waldo, and McKusick 1992).

In the United States, two segments of the population have been singled out for special consideration—the elderly and the poor. While the programs addressing these two groups provide, to some degree, financial access to care, the two groups are treated differently in that their access cards readily identify them. Neither group is integrated into the mainstream through the private insurance mechanism that predominates in the system.

In addition, a large number of people—estimates vary from 34 million to 40 million—have no financial access to care. The very fact that this exists in the United States demonstrates the strong libertarian undertones.

On the other hand, the Canadian system is financed almost entirely through general revenues, with the provincial government contributing the greatest proportion and the federal government transferring revenues from the national coffers in indirect proportion to the provinces' wealth. That is to say, the wealthier the province, the less it receives in transfer funds (Sutherland and Fulton 1992). There is some private health insurance for services above and beyond those guaranteed to all citizens: approximately 25 percent of the total health care expenditures in Canada, for at least the last 15 years, were from private sources (Health and Welfare Canada 1990). The single-source financing of the Canadian system is often cited as one of its greatest strengths. It certainly has the effect of reducing the administrative overhead in the system and unquestionably is more egalitarian than the U.S. system with its myriad of third parties in the private sector.

In the U.S. system, physician reimbursement is almost entirely on a fee-for-service basis. Some physicians are involved with staff-model health maintenance organizations (HMOs) and receive a salary, and of course, hospital-based physicians generally receive a salary. On the whole, U.S. physicians are reimbursed fee-for-service based on fee schedules set by the various third parties. The fiscal intermediaries employed by the federal and state governments for the Medicare and Medicaid programs are instrumental in this process. Private health insurers, often the same organizations that act as the fiscal intermediaries, negotiate fee schedules on behalf of their enrollees.

Beginning in 1992, the U.S. Medicare system introduced a fee system based on the resource-based relative value scale (RBRVS) developed by William Hsiao and his colleagues at Harvard University (Hsaio et al. 1988). This is an attempt to rationalize the physician fee schedule based on the relative resource intensity of each service included in the schedule and, as such, is analogous to setting a market price.

Since 1983, hospitals in the U.S. system have generally been reimbursed on a per case basis. Private payers and state governments followed the lead of the federal government, which introduced the diagnosis-related groups (DRG)–based prospective payment system (PPS) in October 1983. The reimbursement amount for each patient within a classification category is predetermined and is identical for each patient within the category. In effect, this system establishes a quasi "market price," and the hospitals strive to provide the care at a cost that is within a predetermined reimbursement amount (Smith and Fottler 1985). Although the various third parties can ratchet the price upward or downward, once the price is established, the system is a very competitive one. In other words, provider reimbursement in the U.S. system is influenced by fairly strong libertarian values.

Physician reimbursement in the Canadian system is also generally fee-for-service. The fee schedule is negotiated by the physicians in conjunction with the provincial government. This is no different from the method employed in the United States except that the provincial government is the payer and, therefore, the negotiating party in Canada. Some provinces have recently negotiated a total income cap on individual physicians, while others have capped the total physician budget for the province.

Hospitals in the Canadian system are reimbursed by way of a yearly global budget. These budgets are usually determined by simply updating the previous year's budget. Interestingly enough, this egalitarian approach to hospital funding was used by many third party payers in the United States prior to the introduction of DRG-based PPS. In addition, at least two Canadian provinces have introduced adjustments at the margin in hospital budgets based on productivity measures that incorporate case-mix measures (Ontario Hospital Association 1990; Jacobs et al. 1992).

The Canadian reimbursement system is more egalitarian in nature than the U.S. system, but the difference is not nearly as marked as it is with the financing of the systems. There are signs at this time that, in terms of reimbursing the providers, the two countries are moving closer together.

Resource allocation

The distribution of physicians in the United States has been criticized for its lack of congruence with the need for their services. Graphic presentations of the relationship between the number of physicians and the need for their services, as determined by bed days disability, reveal a strong negative relationship (Donabedian et al. 1986). On the other hand, when income per capita is substituted for need, the relationship is strongly positive (Donabedian et al. 1986). Given the ability of physicians to generate demand for their services and, to some extent, control prices, their location is more often determined by the same motives that persuade any other member of society to locate in a given area—motives considered to describe quality of life. As a result, there are many areas in the United States and Canada that can be characterized as underserved and many characterized as overserved. With very little effort to link physician education with the population's need for their services, a physician surplus is likely to develop. The libertarian stance on this is that a surplus will lead to greater competition and lower prices.

Although certificate-of-need (CON) programs exist in some states, their success might be questioned. Pauly (1988) points out that studies comparing states with CON programs with those without have failed to find any effect on total capital investment. He also argues that the evidence suggests that CON programs tended to be captured by the hospitals they were intended to regulate. The duplication of facilities and, to a much greater extent, technology, are characteristics of the system. The lack of controls has resulted in excess bed capacity and underused high-tech equipment. Many hospitals are running below 50 percent occupancy, and many small and rural hospitals have closed as the environment became more competitive when the DRG-based PPS was introduced (Health Insurance Association of America 1990; Mullner 1986).

Linking physician education with need in Canada resulted in a ratio of primary care physicians to specialists of 1:1, compared to 1:7 in the United States. Canadian physicians are free to locate wherever they choose within the jurisdiction of the licensing body (the province), with the knowledge that underserved and overserved areas exist. However, when physicians choose to relocate to another province, they are not automatically granted the right to practice: they can be refused a billing number, which prevents them from seeing patients since the government is the sole payer. The ability of physicians to generate demand for their services also prevails in the Canadian system, and the similarity to the U.S. system is further highlighted by the fact that there is evidence of an oversupply of physicians and talk of increasing the number of specialists relative to primary care physicians (Barer and Stoddart 1991).

In the Canadian hospital sector, the control influenced by provincial government global budgeting has resulted in very little unused bed capacity, less duplication of high-tech equipment, and greater sharing of services.

In terms of resource distribution, the Canadian and U.S. systems are very much alike in that they reflect a libertarian approach to physician distribution. In the hospital sector, however, the Canadian system reflects a more egalitarian approach than that of the United States. Table 2.2 summarizes these differences.

Earlier we suggested that the libertarian might very well say, "let the market take care of the delivery of medical care." We

Table 2.2 Summary of U.S. and Canadian Medical Care System Characteristics

	U.S. System	Canadian System
System funding	Private 40% Public 60%	Private 25% Public 75%
Mode of practice	Small-group, private entrepreneur	Small-group, private entrepreneur
Hospitals	Investor-owned 14% Nongovt. NFP 58% Government 28%	Investor-owned 5% Nongovt. NFP 52% Government 43%
Physician reimbursement	Fee-for-service	Fee-for-service
Hospital reimbursement	Per case	Global budget with some per case adjustment
Physician location	Freedom to practice anywhere within licensing jurisdiction	Freedom to practice anywhere within licensing jurisdiction

might suggest at this point that the rallying cry of the egalitarian is, "health care is a right." The above, very cursory examination of the medical systems in the United States and Canada would indicate a greater libertarian influence in the United States and a greater egalitarian influence in Canada. In fact, the federal government in Canada has mandated that health care coverage be universal, comprehensive, accessible, portable (between provinces), and publicly administered (Hatcher, Hatcher, and Hatcher 1985). In summation, we must recognize that a mandate such as this put forth by the Canadian government could not have emanated from the representatives of a society with very strong libertarian values. Without some form of dictatorship, it would not be possible for a particular government to persuade its citizens to conform to a mandate that did not reflect society's values. This was demonstrated dramatically in the United States when the catastrophic amendment to the Medicare Act was repealed in 1989 after only a few months, in response to the overwhelming objections by the elderly in the population. The amendment provided for, among other things, additional long-term care and out-of-hospital prescription drugs. However, the funding of these additional benefits was through a surtax levied on the Medicare eligibles. Rovner (1990) points out that "nothing gets the attention of Congress faster than unhappy senior citizens."

Discussion Questions

1. Universality in a health insurance or prepayment plan indicates that all members of the population are included. What might be the positions of the egalitarians and libertarians on this issue?

2. Comprehensivity indicates that all medical care services would be included in a health insurance plan. What might be the positions of the egalitarians and libertarians on this issue?

3. First-dollar coverage in a health insurance plan indicates that medical care services are free at the point of consumption. What might be the positions of the egalitarians and libertarians on this issue?

Note

1. Any introductory economic text will discuss this principle in detail.

References

American Hospital Association. *AHA Statistics, 1993–1994*. Chicago: AHA, 1993.

Barer, M. L., and G. L. Stoddart. *Toward Integrated Medical Resource Policies for Canada*. Vancouver: Center for Health Services and Policy Research, University of British Columbia, 1991.

Burner, S. T., D. R. Waldo, and D. R. McKusick. "National Health Expenditure Projections Through 2030." *Health Care Financing Review* 14 (Fall 1992): 1–29.

Canadian Hospital Association. *Guide to Canadian Health Care Facilities*. Ottawa, Ontario: CHA, 1993.

Donabedian, A. *Aspects of Medical Care Administration: Specifying Requirements for Health Care*. Cambridge, MA: Harvard University Press for The Commonwealth Fund, 1973.

————. "Social Responsibility for Personal Health Services: An Examination of Basic Values." *Inquiry* 8 (June 1971): 3–19.

Donabedian, A., S. J. Axelrod, L. Wyszewianski, and R. L. Lichtenstein. *Medical Care Chartbook*, 8th ed. Ann Arbor, MI: Health Administration Press, 1986.

Feldstein, P. J. *Health Care Economics*, 3d ed. New York: John Wiley & Sons, 1988.

Ferguson, C. E., and S. C. Maurice. *Economic Analysis*. Homewood, IL: Richard D. Irwin Inc., 1970.

Friedman, M. *Capitalism and Freedom*. Chicago: University of Chicago Press, 1962.

Hatcher, G. H., P. R. Hatcher, and E. C. Hatcher. "Health services in Canada." In *Comparative Health Systems*, edited by M. W. Raffel. University Park: Pennsylvania State University Press, 1985.

Health Insurance Association of America. *Source Book of Health Insurance Data 1990*. Washington, DC: HIAA, 1990.

Health and Welfare Canada. Health Information Division of the Policy. Planning and Information Branch of the Department of National Health and Welfare Canada. *National Health Expenditures in Canada, 1975–1987*. Ottawa, Ontario: Health and Welfare Canada, 1990.

Hsiao, W. C., P. Braun, D. Yntema, and E. R. Becker. "Estimating Physicians' Work for a Resource-Based Relative-Value Scale." *New England Journal of Medicine* 319 (September 1988): 835–41.

Jacobs, P., E. M. Hall, J. R. Lave, and M. Glendining. "Alberta's Acute Care Funding Project." *Healthcare Management Forum* 5 (Fall 1992): 4–11.

Mullner, R. "Hospital Closures, Mergers and Consolidations." Presented at the Third Annual Meeting of the Association of Health Services Research, June 1986.

Ontario Hospital Association. *Hospital Funding in Transition: Report on Phase I of the Transitional Funding Initiative*. Don Mills, Ontario: The Association, 1990.

Pauly, M. V. "A Primer on Competition in Medical Markets." In *Health Care in America*, edited by H. E. Frech III. San Francisco: Pacific Research Institute for Public Policy, 1988.

Rovner, J. "Climbing Medigap Premiums Draw Attention on the Hill." *Congressional Quarterly* (17 February 1990): 527–31.

Smith, H. L., and M. D. Fottler. *Prospective Payment: Managing for Operational Effectiveness*. Rockville, MD: Aspen Systems Corporation, 1985.

Sutherland, R. W., and M. J. Fulton. *Health Care in Canada*. Ottawa. Ontario: Canadian Public Health Association, 1992.

Figure 3.1 A Conceptual Model of the Medical Care System

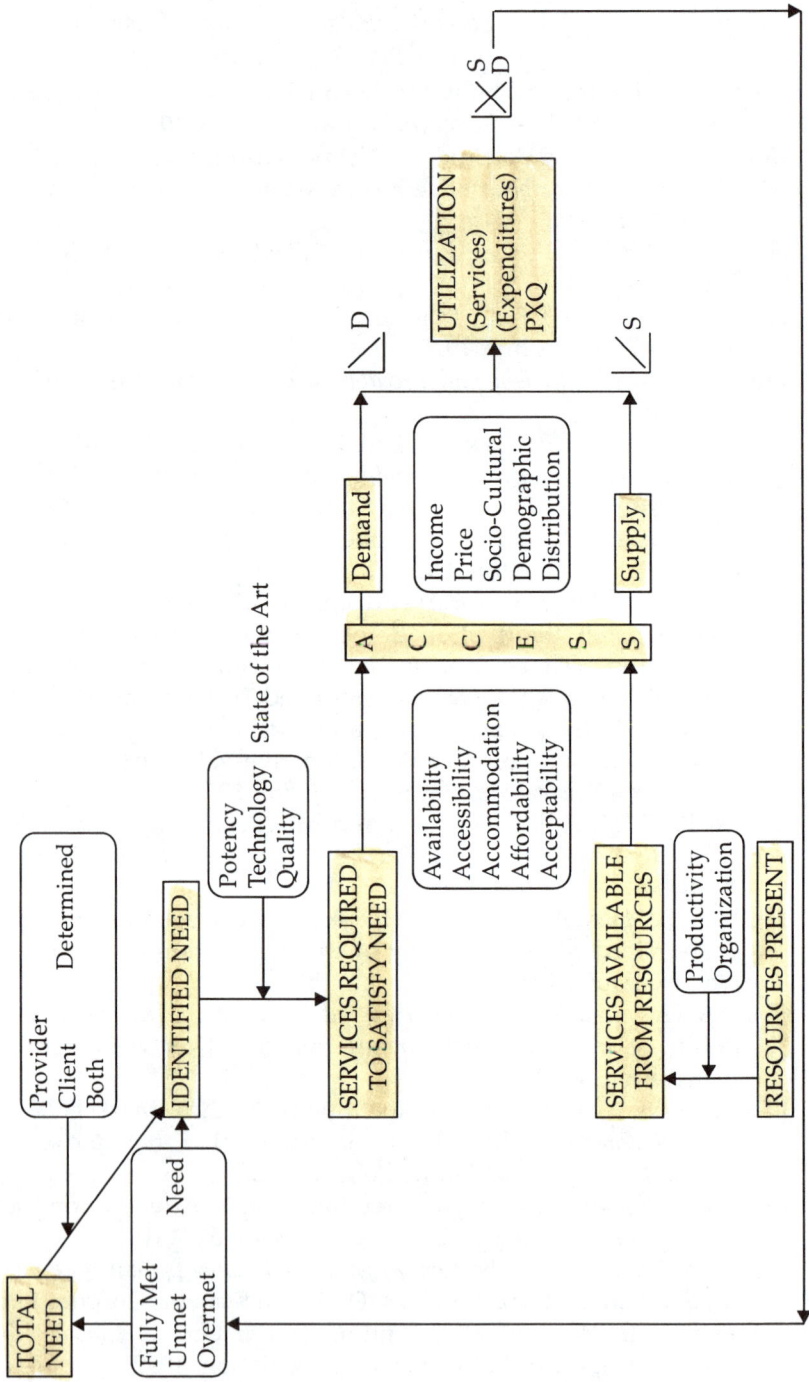

Chapter 3

A Conceptual Model of the Medical Care System: An Introduction

In the interest of imposing order on the immense, and often fragmented, body of literature in the field of medical care, it is necessary to develop a conceptual frame of reference. In the absence of an acceptable theory of medical care, a generalizable, conceptual model serves as a reasonable substitute. Donabedian's groundbreaking work *Aspects of Medical Care Administration* (1973) provides the substance and detail for such a model. Figure 3.1 is a model introduced as the framework for all that follows in this text. Each of the following chapters will comprehensively explore one of the components of this model.

This chapter is a walk through the model, an opportunity to briefly explain the model and to clarify the terminology.

Beginning in the upper lefthand corner, *total need* represents a somewhat abstract concept of need in any population—that is, we can state confidently, a priori, that there is a need for medical care in any population. The abstract quality of this concept derives from understanding that in the event an entire population were examined and no need uncovered, it could still be argued that need is present although, given the current state of the art, need cannot be detected.

Identified need, then, is the need that can be detected and as such, is the only level of need that can be addressed to some extent by the medical care system. The model allows for both a client-defined need or *felt* need, and a provider-defined or *clinical* need or a combination of both. What is important here is that the two definitions of need may be incongruent, thereby presenting society with the dilemma of which need the medical care system will be designed to address. In some cases, society itself defines need. Our model lends itself to considering that society may very well select among the sets of provider- and client-defined needs in order to establish priorities for the medical care system. In other words, societal needs are simply an attempt to prioritize needs as seen by the provider *and* the client.

Need having been identified, the number and type of *services required* can be determined given the current state of the art. *State of the art* includes the current level of technology, its ability to eliminate or prevent from worsening the identified need level (potency), and the quality level with which it is applied. Poor quality could result equally in a greater or fewer number of services required. For example, if for a particular condition, an acceptable level of quality requires that four office visits be provided, a provider of poor quality may require only two visits or as many as six. Poor quality can be either service-increasing or service-reducing.

Moving to the bottom of the model, *resources present* represents the raw numbers of resources presently available to the medical care system. Such things as the number of physicians, other personnel, and beds are included in this component of the model without regard for their service-producing capabilities.

A reduction or increase in the number of available resources would probably result in a reduction or increase in the number of services available, but not necessarily on a one-for-one basis. The number of *services available from resources* is dependent on the organization and the productivity of the resources. It is not too difficult to conceive of a situation where the same number of resources generated more services under one type of organization than under another type of organization.

Access is considered the modifying concept between services required and services available. In addition, the extent to which access is achieved is the extent to which there is utilization. Although the number and type of services available might be identical to the number and type of services required, care may not be received by those who need it due to one or several barriers to access.

Services required to treat identifiable need and services available from the resources in the system, when modified by access, are major factors in *demand* and *supply*, respectively. Only when access is achieved is the action of the client demanding and provider supplying a service actually consummated. The interaction of demand and supply results in *utilization*, according to the model. Classic economic theory refers to this as the "quantity willingly demanded" and the "quantity willingly supplied." An important difference, however, between medical care services and many others is that, as discussed in Chapter 2, consumers of medical care cannot be characterized as rational consumers. Medical care is not "willingly" demanded[1] (McConnell 1972).

Services utilized can now be compared with services required to satisfy need. The difference between these two translates into *unmet need* (when services required are greater than services utilized), *fully met need* (when services required are identical to services utilized), and *overmet need* (when services required are less than services utilized). The notion of unmet need is extended as shown in the model to include need that currently cannot be identified—that is, undiscovered need or the difference between *total need* and *utilization* is included in the concept, even though it is not, of course, quantifiable.

A conceptual model, such as the one presented here, allows a comprehensive analysis of the effect of specific changes to particular components of the model. For example, the effect of removing one of the existing barriers to access can be traced throughout the system, thereby avoiding the tendency to consider only the initial impact. The model also greatly facilitates policy analysis, in that government intervention of all kinds can be unequivocally located on the model. For example, HMO legislation (P.L. 93-222) (see Luft 1980) and the National Health Planning and Resource Development Act (P.L. 93-641) (see Klarman 1978) clearly were designed to affect organization, while Medicare (Social Security Act, Title 18) and Medicaid (Social Security Act, Title 19) (see Richardson 1980) were designed to affect access.

Theory is defined in the dictionary as "a plausible or scientifically acceptable general principle or body of principles offered to explain phenomena." If a conceptual model is to be accepted as a reasonable substitute in the absence of a theory, the true test of that model rests in its generalizability. The model presented here offers an explanation, not only of the medical care system as a whole, but of individual components of the medical care and health care systems. It simply requires that the specific need be identified and that the resources considered be those that can address the particular need in question. For example, the model can be used to explain the use of public health services, individual preventive care services, or services that address individual chronic or acute disease conditions.

Since the medical care delivery system might be considered part of the service industry, the applicability of the model to services in general can be explored without trivializing the medical care system. Take the automobile repair industry as an analogue, although other sectors of the repair industry would serve equally well.

In this analogy, the customer recognizes a need for a service, perhaps a regular maintenance checkup. The maintenance professional then either confirms or discounts the need for the service(s). The resources available to the automobile service industry include among others, the number of trained mechanics, that are capable of delivering a certain number and type of service. The number of services is contingent on the organization and productivity of these resources. Therefore, the five components of access as defined in the model (availability, accessibility, accommodation, affordability, acceptability) apply. A service transaction will not occur unless the customer finds the right kind of service *available*. For example, suppose foreign car service was required but only mechanics for domestic cars are available. In addition, the service location must be geographically *accessible*, open at convenient times (*accommodation*), staffed with competent, courteous, and friendly people (*acceptability*), and have reasonable prices (*affordability*).

The model might also serve as a graphic presentation of the variables that constitute a demand and supply function. In classic economics, consumer choice or demand is dependent on consumer wants supported by the ability to pay. Within their ability to pay, consumers demand services relative to the potential for the services to satisfy their wants[2] (Hibdon 1969). This idea of consuming to satisfy wants is referred to as consumer "taste" by economists[3] (Ferguson and Maurice 1970).

In the medical care application of the model, the variable "need" can be equated with "want" in a nonmedical care service setting: the clients are interested in satisfying their need for care. Need and want can be reconciled under the rubric of "taste" in a demand function. In other words, if the definition of "taste" is broadened to include "a propensity toward," we can assume that an individual with a broken leg has a taste for orthopedic services. The only problem with this analogy is that it is difficult to conceive of a taste that is not recognized by the consumer. However, since the medical care system very rarely addresses a need that is not first recognized by the client, the model would seem to fit reasonably well.

In Chapters 4–10, each of the model's components will be discussed in detail. Chapter 11 will then examine the generalizability of the model to demonstrate its applicability to all levels and types of care and its utility in the examination of policy decisions.

Discussion Questions

1. Select one article from each of three scholarly journals in the health care field. What component of the conceptual model does the research address and what possible implications (components of the model) does the model identify that the author(s) have overlooked?

2. Consider the courses in your program of study in the health care field. How does each course fit in the conceptual model?

Notes

1. Any introductory text on the principles of economics will discuss this in detail.
2. Any introductory microeconomics text will discuss this principle in detail.
3. Any introductory economics text will discuss this principle in detail.

References

Donabedian, A. *Aspects of Medical Care Administration: Specifying Requirements for Health Care*. Cambridge, MA: Harvard University Press for the Commonwealth Fund, 1973.

Ferguson , C. E., and S. C. Maurice. *Economic Analysis*. Homewood, IL: Richard D. Irwin Inc., 1970.

Hibdon, J. E., *Price and Welfare Theory*. New York: McGraw-Hill Book Company, 1969.

Klarman, H. E. "Health Planning: Progress, Prospects, and Issues." *Milbank Memorial Fund Quarterly/Health and Society* 56 (Winter 1978): 78–112.

Luft, H. S. *Health Maintenance Organizations: Dimensions of Performance*. New York: Wiley-Interscience, 1980.

McConnell, C. R. *Economics: Principles, Problems, and Policies*, 5th ed. New York: McGraw Hill, 1972.

Richardson, W. C. "Financing Health Services." In *Introduction to Health Services*, edited by S. J. Williams and P. R. Torrens. New York: John Wiley & Sons, 1980.

Figure 4.1 Need and Identified Need

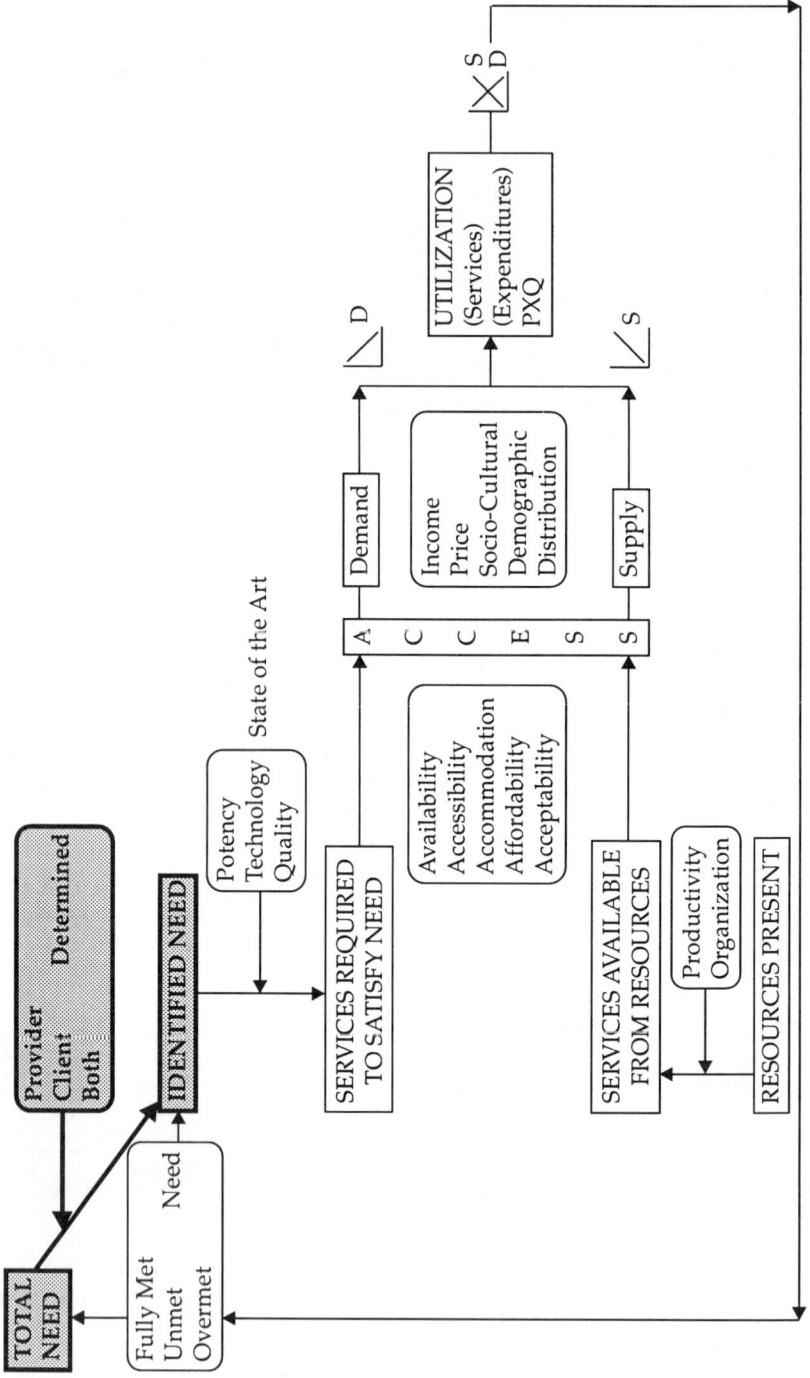

TOTAL NEED

Provider
Client — Determined
Both

IDENTIFIED NEED

Fully Met
Unmet — Need
Overmet

Potency
Technology — State of the Art
Quality

SERVICES REQUIRED
TO SATISFY NEED

Availability
Accessibility
Accommodation
Affordability
Acceptability

A
C
C
E
S
S

Demand

Income
Price
Socio-Cultural
Demographic
Distribution

Supply

SERVICES AVAILABLE
FROM RESOURCES

Productivity
Organization

RESOURCES PRESENT

UTILIZATION
(Services)
(Expenditures)
PXQ

D

S

$\times \begin{matrix} S \\ D \end{matrix}$

Chapter 4

The Need for Medical Care

If pressed to answer the question, Why does any medical care system exist? an obvious answer might be "to address the need for medical care in the population it serves." Although obvious, this answer certainly should not be interpreted as unenlightened or frivolous. Indeed, such a simple concept lies at the very core of any medical care system and provides the parameters by which systems are judged and compared.

This chapter describes the various levels of need for care, ranging from undetectable need to provider-determined need, to client-determined need. The lack of agreement or congruence between provider and client in assessing need will be examined and explained. The various measures of need adopted will be introduced and followed by more detailed descriptions of two classic studies on the measurement of need. Finally, the three reasons for measuring need are discussed. To maintain the continuity implicit in the systemwide, conceptual approach at the heart of this text, the part of the model under discussion in this chapter is highlighted by the shading in the model on the opposite page.

A logical extension of the argument that the medical care system exists to address the need for medical care would be that if there were no need for medical care, there would be no need for a medical care system. However unlikely it is that such a state of equilibrium would ever exist, this idea is acceptable as a state toward which the ideal medical care system tends to move. In other words, it is a dynamic rather than a steady state system where both the need for care and the ability to provide care constantly change.

Following Donabedian (1973), this point can be clarified by considering the "iceberg" phenomenon first proposed by Gordon (1950), later adopted by others (for example, Last 1963), and consistent with the work of Winter and Metzner (1958), who introduced the concepts of undetectable need, detectable need, felt need, and absolute need (see Figure 4.2). It is called the iceberg phenomenon because only the tip of the need for care is exposed above the surface, or clinical horizon. As with an iceberg, a much greater amount of need lies undetectable below the surface.

Now let us examine a given population—any clearly definable population such as a cohort of students, all students at a given university, the residents of a village or town, or the population of the country. It might be easier to understand this concept if our hypothetical population is small. Because our population is small, we can survey it by visiting all members and asking them if they feel they are in need of medical care. A word of caution: an individual's perception of need for care is subjective and might be

Figure 4.2   The Iceberg Phenomenon

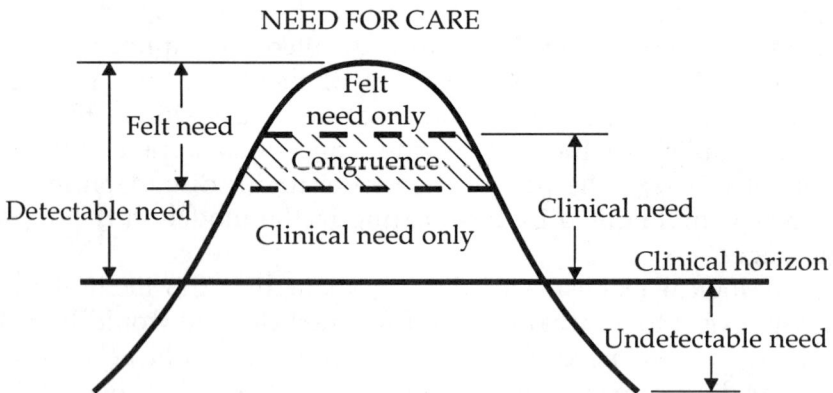

NEED FOR CARE

Note: Adapted from Avedis Donabedian, *Aspects of Medical Care Administration: Specifying Requirements for Health Care.* Reprinted by permission of Harvard University Press, Cambridge, MA. © 1973.

as simple as wanting someone to whom they can talk about their feelings. The answers the survey generates can be quantified to establish the felt need in this population, if any exists.

After surveying the population, we convene all of the leading clinical diagnosticians together with all the necessary support personnel and equipment. For the sake of this example, let us assume that every possible diagnostic test and procedure known to medical practitioners anywhere is known to our practitioners and that the equipment and facilities necessary to perform those tests are available to them. In other words, these practitioners are state-of-the-art practitioners. The clinical experts will then examine each member of the population as thoroughly as currently possible. By quantifying their results, the clinical need in the population is established, if it exists.

Three important points emerge from this iceberg phenomenon. The first is the relationship among the state of the art, the clinical horizon, and the dynamic nature of the medical care system. Recall that equilibrium was the state toward which an ideal medical care system tends to move, as well as the state where all medical care needs are met. The state of the art, in terms of diagnostic procedures and technologies, determines the clinical horizon. The iceberg phenomenon shown in Figure 4.2 indicates that as the state of the art improves, the clinical horizon is pushed downward to expose more need in the population; this does not necessarily mean that state-of-the-art ability to successfully treat disease keeps pace with state-of-the-art ability to discover disease. Hence, even in a state where all need was currently satisfied, at some point the clinical horizon would be further depressed and more disease would be exposed.

The second point is that of congruence between felt need and clinical need. In Figure 4.2, clinical need overlaps with felt need, and the extent of the overlap represents the extent to which clients and providers agree on the need for care, or more accurately put, the extent to which client felt (or determined) need is clinically confirmed by the provider. This is not to suggest that need that is not clinically confirmed is not real. On the contrary, if clients feel they need care, they do in fact need care. The questions then become, What type of care? and Who should provide it?

From Figure 4.2 note that when there is less than 100 percent congruence, two other categories of need are possible—felt need only and clinical need only.

The third point is raised by recognizing these two categories and is best captured by the question, What need should any society be prepared to fund and provide facilities for? If it were determined to be wise to develop a system to address all of the detectable need in the population, unless all of the population were medically examined, the system would have surplus capacity as measured by the component *clinical need only*. Consider the cost to examine every single member of a given population, or even a substantial portion of it. On the other hand, recommending that a system address all felt need in the population encourages misuse of the system. That is, the system would be attempting to treat conditions for which there was no clinical basis and therefore no medical solution. It follows then that, absent the resources to examine the total population for every pathology currently known or to treat need without a clinical basis, a medical care system should have the facilities to address that need on which both the client and the provider agree—that is, the shaded component of the iceberg shown in Figure 4.2.

This notion of *congruence* is extremely important in any medical care system that relies on the client to first feel a need for care. Since it is difficult to conceive of a system that does not have this dependency, further examination of this concept is in order. The amount of congruence will vary according to the type of disease condition and the socioeconomic status of the client. To illustrate the variation according to disease condition, we call on the data compiled by Sanders (1962) from the findings of the Commission on Chronic Illness and cited by Donabedian (1973). For certain disease conditions, Sanders (1962) reported the prevalence of the condition as reported by survey respondents and by physicians after clinical examination. The data show the number of clients who believe they have the condition and the number for whom it is clinically confirmed. For the purpose of this example, only selected results are presented in Table 4.1.

The number of cases that were clinically confirmed is standardized to 100. In Table 4.1 that number is derived by adding column 2—the number who did not think the condition existed but a physician did and column 3—the number of clients who thought

Table 4.1   Client-Perceived Need, Clinically Confirmed Need, and Congruence for Selected Conditions

Condition	Client Only (1)	Physician Only (2)	Client and Physician (3)	True Positives (4)
Asthma/hay fever	48%	18%	82%	63%
Diabetes	2	62	38	95
Heart condition	9	85	15	63
Peptic ulcer	23	95	5	18

Note: Adapted from Avedis Donabedian, *Aspects of Medical Care Administration: Specifying Requirements for Health Care.* Reprinted by permission of Harvard University Press, Cambridge, MA. © 1973.
    Source: Sanders 1962.

the condition existed and a physician confirmed it. Column 3 indicates congruence, and considering the variance in disease conditions, it is not surprising that it varies from 5 to 82 percent. Table 4.1 also shows, for example, that for every 100 cases of peptic ulcer in a population, 28 people (23 + 5) would present themselves to the system, all other things being equal. Only five of those cases would be clinically confirmed, and perhaps more alarmingly, 95 cases would be missed unless 100 percent of the population were examined.

It might be tempting to interpret the neat monotonic decrease in congruence as representing some measure of the clients' ability to recognize symptoms associated with each particular disease condition. The less common the disease, the less likely the client is to recognize the need for care. However, when considering the number of true positives (column 4)—that is, the number of times a client's belief is substantiated by a physician—the order of things changes somewhat. Column 4 shows that in this population, 95 percent of those clients who think they have diabetes would have this confirmed. Similarly, only 63 percent of those who think they have asthma/hay fever would have it confirmed. Peptic ulcer still remains at the bottom of this list, indicating perhaps that clients are the least knowledgeable about this disease condition. Nevertheless, even though the overall ordering does not prevail, these data demonstrate that congruence varies by disease condition.

To examine the variation in congruence that can be attributed to the difference in the socioeconomic level of the client, the work of Donabedian (1973), which includes Koos's classic work *The Health of Regionville* (1954), will be utilized. Table 4.2 presents selected portions of the data from these works.

To interpret Table 4.2, it is necessary to accept that for all of the conditions mentioned, physicians would agree that everyone should consult a physician. That being the case, columns 1 and 3 (Perceived) indicate the amount of congruence. For blood in the urine, 100 percent of those in the higher socioeconomic group indicated that they should consult a physician, thereby showing complete congruence. On the other hand, only 69 percent of the lower socioeconomic group agreed that a physician should be consulted. Compare column 3 with column 1 to see the difference (31 to 59 percent) in the amount of congruence between the two levels of socioeconomic status for the same condition (column 3 subtracted from column 1). Higher socioeconomic status referred to those with higher incomes who were generally employed in one of the professions. Lower status referred to those with incomes approximately one-fifth of those in the higher status who were generally employed sporadically for an hourly wage.

These data were taken from a study that asked the respondents whether they should see a physician for the symptom in

Table 4.2 Perceived Need, Actual Need, and Congruence for Selected Conditions

Condition	Higher Socioeconomic Status		Lower Socioeconomic Status	
	Perceived (1)	Actual (2)	Perceived (3)	Actual (4)
Blood in urine	100%	100%	69%	80%
Loss of weight	80	100	21	45
Fainting spells	80	82	33	56

Note: Adapted from Avedis Donabedian, *Aspects of Medical Care Administration: Specifying Requirements for Health Care*. Reprinted by permission of Harvard University Press, Cambridge, MA. © 1973.
Source: Koos 1954.

question. In Table 4.2, this is labeled "perceived," indicating "perceived need," so the congruence highlighted should more correctly be referred to as the congruence between client-perceived need and physician-determined need. In columns 2 and 4, the data were taken from a study that identified those with the symptom in question and asked whether they were receiving care. In Table 4.2, this is labeled "actual," indicating "actual need," and the congruence identified reflects the congruence between client-actual need and physician-determined need. Congruence in the concrete (actual) is greater than congruence in the abstract (perceived), although these were for two different populations.

Although from the examples presented here it appears to be possible to have 100 percent congruence for certain conditions, this is not likely. This may be somewhat intuitive, but a more formal discussion of client need and provider need will provide the rationale for the possible lack of congruence.

Client-defined need

From the clients' perspective, the need for care is more likely to be based on the subjective determination that they need immediate relief for a condition they are experiencing. They are not generally motivated by the concern for what will happen in the future if they do not receive treatment. Even in cases where informed clients might be aware of the adverse consequences of delaying treatment, they are often more persuaded by the answer to the self-imposed question, How do I feel, now?

This type of need has been variably referred to as subjective, desired, nonscientific, and felt, and it is extremely difficult to quantify. It can, however, be characterized as (1) need that has no pathological basis, (2) need that has a pathological basis and would be clinically confirmed if the client submitted to an examination, or (3) need that has a pathological basis but the state-of-the-art technology is not capable of identifying it (i.e., it is below the clinical horizon). By definition, it is impossible to distinguish between the first and third categories, and unfortunately, it makes no difference in terms of providing care in the short run because the medical care system cannot treat the condition.

Provider-defined need

From the providers' perspective, need is generally defined in terms of microscopic or gross changes in the structure of body cells, body tissue, and the chemical composition of body fluids. Providers are more concerned with the clinical progression of disease, or what will happen in the future if the condition is not treated. This type of need has been variably referred to as objective, required, scientific, and clinical, and it is much more readily quantified within the constraints of the state of the art.

Those who argue that the only relevant need is clinically confirmed need may have a good point, since it's the only need that has any chance of being addressed. On the other hand, repeated unconfirmed need may serve to prompt clinical research in the area, and the failure to discover any pathological basis for the need as presented may, in fact, be treatment enough.

Measuring Need

Having described the two perspectives on the need for care, we now turn our discussion to determining the magnitude of need. The first order of business is to decide what is to be included in the metric. Donabedian (1973) refers to this as the scope of measurement.

At this point, recall the WHO definition of good health: "complete physical, psychological, and social well-being" (Somers and Somers 1977). An important point to make is that we really do not know how to measure health; we measure illness. (In fact, note that health insurance is in actuality illness insurance.) To pursue the WHO definition of good health, then some measure of physical illness, psychological illness, and social illness must be included. This is a difficult order, and one that the medical care system, as we generally conceive it, is not in a position to address. We have defined the medical care system as the day-to-day, one-on-one delivery of medical care that does not include medical research, public health, or other nonmedical contributors to improved health status. With this in mind, let us consider some of the types of information that might be used in measuring need, its availability, usefulness, and limitations.

- *Population count.* The number of people in a population is sometimes used as a crude measure of need in that population. The idea behind this notion is, *all other things being equal*, a population of 1 million will need twice as much medical care as a population of 500,000. The problem with this, of course, is that all other things are very seldom equal. Yet this fact does not prevent us from using this approach to measuring need in estimating the number of physicians and beds required in a given population. For example, implicit in the use of physician-to-population ratios in determining underserved areas is accepting that the same number of physicians is required for every unit of every population, regardless of the characteristics of the population. In other words, if 200 physicians per 100,000 population is the accepted normative standard, all population must have the equivalent of 200 physicians per 100,000 population or be designated as underserved. Population data are readily available from the census.

- *Population count plus demographics.* An age- and sex-specific population count is more informative than a simple population count regarding need in a given population. Knowing, for example, that a population is elderly or predominantly female (or male) is useful in measuring need and helps in making at least some of the other things equal. These data can also be found in the census.

- *Mortality data.* The number of deaths per 1,000 population, especially when used in conjunction with demographics and disease, is generally accepted as a measure of need in a given population. Age-, sex-, and disease-specific death rates are also readily available. While certainly some deaths result from the lack of needed medical care, many others are the result of factors outside the realm of medical care. For example, a high death rate may be an indication of the lack of adequate housing, food, or sanitation— none of which can be addressed by the medical care system.

- *Morbidity data.* Data on the extent of morbidity and situations requiring care are the most definitive in terms of measuring need; they are also the most difficult to obtain. The methods used to collect and analyze such data are costly and time-consuming. National or population-specific surveys, vital records and registries, medical records reviews, and screening are examples of data-gathering techniques.

Numerous attempts utilizing many different methodologies have been made to measure need. One common technique is to use incidence (new cases of a given disease or condition), prevalence (amount of a given disease or condition at any one time), or mortality rates (age-, sex-, and disease-specific deaths for every 1,000 members of the population). These data may be obtained for whole populations or subpopulations and may focus on one or several disease conditions. The magnitude of these various indices are interpreted as the level of need in the population.

One cannot quarrel with the premise that the presence of a given disease condition represents a need for medical care. To accept these indices as valid measures of total need permits acceptance that a population with a greater presence of a specific disease condition has a greater need. We should, of course, question whether these measures capture the total need for care.

A good example of the use of incidence and prevalence to establish need in a population can be found in the classic work of Lee and Jones (1933), who set out to establish, among other things, how many primary care physicians were required in the United States by first determining the amount of need in the population. As part of their measurement of need, they determined the incidence and prevalence of 95 major categories of conditions requiring diagnosis and treatment and established an expectancy rate per 1,000. For example, the category of Diseases of the Ear and Mastoid Process included otitis media, earache, mastoid diseases, and all other and had an expectancy rate of 15.0.

Lee and Jones (1933) went on to establish standards for treatment that were translated first into service equivalents and then into time equivalents. From the total time requirements, they were able to determine the number of physicians required by dividing the total time by the time available to a typical physician.

The definition of need used by Lee and Jones (1933) was derived from a clinically determined norm and could be said to include a measure of physical well-being only. (Other more recent studies have addressed incidence and prevalence; the Lee and Jones study is cited because although dated, expresses the concept best.)

Measures of need that include other components of well-being require much more costly methods of data gathering and generally can only be applied to small subgroups of the population. Survey research techniques, which include population sampling, questionnaire development, and the interview process, are central to gathering the type of data required in developing such a measure of need. Many eminent scholars have explored the possibility of measuring need in a manner that approaches some of the components of the WHO's definition of good health (see Chapter 1). This has resulted in a wealth of information on health status measures. For example, Katz et al. (1963) developed the Index of ADL (activities of daily living) as a measure of health in the elderly and chronically ill. Schonfeld, Heston, and Falk (1972) replicated the Lee and Jones study, measuring need to determine the number of primary care providers. Patrick, Bush, and Chen (1973) developed a social construct of health employing two dimensions, function level and prognosis. Mossey and Shapiro (1982) found that self-rated health in the elderly was a predictor of mortality and, therefore, a reasonable health status measure. More recently, the excellent work of the scholars involved in the classic Rand Health Insurance Experiment have provided us with health status measures (Ware et al. 1980; Eisen et al. 1980; Davies and Ware 1981; Stewart, Ware, and Brook 1982).

To avoid presenting a literature review and to provide the reader with a sense of the complex nature of what might, at first, appear to be a simple concept, two classic works on health status measures are briefly examined for illustrative purposes.

In one of the earlier works in this field, Lester Breslow (1972) in working with the Human Population Laboratory of Alameda, California, developed an instrument to quantitatively assess health status as defined by the WHO. He constructed three separate measures, one each for physical, mental, and social health.

Physical health

Seven categories of physical health were devised as follows:

1. Disability, severe. Reported trouble with feeding, dressing, climbing stairs, getting outdoors, or [the] inability to work for six months or longer.
2. Disability, less. Did not report above, but reported changing hours or type of work, or cutting down on other activities for six months or longer.
3. Chronic conditions, second level. Did not report any disability, but reported two or more impairments or chronic conditions (list of 12 chronic conditions including heart trouble, asthma, hernia, and 6 impairments given) in the past 12 months.
4. Chronic conditions, first level. Did not report any disability, but reported one chronic condition or impairment in the past 12 months.
5. Symptomatic. Did not report any disability, impairment, or chronic condition but reported one or more symptoms (list of symptoms including tightness in chest, pains in back given).
6. Without complaint, second level. Low to medium energy level—fewer than 3 "high energy" answers to questions.
7. Without complaint, first level. High-energy level—at least 3 "high energy" answers. (Breslow 1972)

Mental health

Mental health was measured in terms of feeling "depressed or very unhappy" or feeling "on top of the world" (Breslow 1972).

Social health

Four categories of social health were devised as follows:

1. Employability—educational achievement, occupational status, and job experience.
2. Marital satisfaction.

3. Sociability—number of "close" friends and relatives.
4. Community involvement—church attendance, political activity, and organizational membership. (Breslow 1972)

Breslow (1972) surveyed a probability sample of 6,928 adults in Alameda County and achieved an 86 percent response rate. From these data he was able to place each person on the axes of physical, mental, and social well-being. No attempt was made to combine these three measures into a single index of health, but it was possible to examine the relationship between various behaviors (and conditions) and the physical, mental, or social well-being of this population.

It is not too difficult to see that merely establishing the health status level of a very small subpopulation using this model is very complex and prohibitively costly. While the results of such an assessment might be vital to the surveyed population, when viewed in the context of the medical care system as defined in this work, they could prove to be frustrating. In other words, this methodology is certain to uncover need that the medical care system cannot address. This is not to criticize the system for failing to address a need, rather to recognize the complexity of the definition of need and the nontrivial notion that the medical care system exists to meet a need. Others have attempted to operationalize the WHO definition of good health as discussed earlier, but the Breslow work, although dated, is a classic example of an excellent attempt.

Fanshell and Bush (1970), in developing a single index of health status, were implicitly concerned with physical, psychological, and social well-being. They suggested a continuum ranging from well-being to death and argued that function is central to any generalized notion of well-being. As a result, they developed the 11 categories shown in Table 4.3 to be used in a health status index.

According to this classification scheme, on any given day it is possible to locate every member of the population in one—and only one—of the 11 states of function. The present functional state of each individual can be measured on a scale of 0 to 1 and summed across all population members.

Since this index relies on an ordinal scale, it suffers from the limitations of all ordinal scales in that the magnitude of the intervals between categories are unknown. In other words, it is

Table 4.3   Continuum of Function/Dysfunction in Health
Status Index

	Function	Dysfunction
Well-being	1.0	0.0
Dissatisfaction	.	.
Discomfort	.	.
Minor disability	.	.
Major disability	.	.
Disabled	.	.
Confined	.	.
Confined (bed-ridden)	.	.
Isolated	.	.
Coma	.	.
Death	0.0	1.0

Note: Adapted from Avedis Donabedian, *Aspects of Medical Care Administration: Specifying Requirements for Health Care*. Reprinted by permission of Harvard University Press, Cambridge, MA. © 1973.
Source: Fanshell and Bush 1970.

impossible to know whether it is better have two people in the population with a dysfunctional level "disabled" or one person who died. There is no doubt that complete well-being represents a functional level of 1.0 and death represents a functional level of 0.0, but the categories between require further weighting. Fanshell and Bush (1970), of course, recognized this and explored several methods of assigning weights to each functional state. These methods are identified as economic, behavioral, survey, and paired comparisons.

Economic methods of weighting draw on the notion that cost to society, or the system, can serve as a measure of the value of each functional state. It also has the advantage of being easily quantifiable. In other words, the number of resources required to move a person from one functional state to the next highest level, or the amount of resources lost as the result of a person remaining in any given state, serves as the weight for that functional state.

Behavioral methods of weighting rely on first determining the number and type of roles performed by each member of the population and then ascribing a relative importance to each role. Clearly, this method relies heavily on value judgment, which can be both a positive and a negative attribute. On the positive side, each population or subpopulation has its own set of social values that can be incorporated in the measurement scale. On the negative side, the weights attained in this manner suffer from an image of being "soft" or lacking in objectivity.

Survey methods of weighting might be considered a variation on the subjective, behavioral method described above. For this method, the population is surveyed and asked to place a value on each functional state. Given that this is a subjective measure, it suffers the same criticism leveled at the behavioral method. Fanshell and Bush (1970) cite Kenneth Arrow's (1963) argument on aggregating individual utility functions to point out that any attempt to aggregate these individual findings requires even further value judgments.

The *paired comparisons* method is yet another subjective measure with, as Fanshell and Bush (1970) suggest, public officials functioning as representatives of society's judgments comparing two functional levels. The decision-maker is asked to compare moving from one functional level to a state of well-being with moving from another functional level to a state of well-being— for example, moving from a state of disability to one of well-being compared with moving from a state of confinement to one of well-being. Weights can then be assigned when all possible combinations have been considered.

Reasons for measuring need

The literature on measuring need is voluminous. The classic studies discussed were used for illustrative purposes to provide the reader with a feel for the complexity of the concept of need for medical care. The purpose for which need is being measured determines how need is measured. Donabedian (1973) suggests three reasons for measuring need—evaluation, estimation, and priority-setting.

Evaluation

By measuring need in the population, we can evaluate how well the medical care system is performing. We can compare one population to another, or we can compare the same population over time and answer such questions as: Are we healthier than population Y? Is our medical care system better than that of population Y? Is our population healthier this year than it was five or ten years ago? Did a newly introduced program of care improve the health status of our population?

The important point here is that an evaluation of the medical care system must be formulated by an understanding of the type of need the system is capable of addressing. There is no point in embarking on an evaluation of the medical care system that employs an elaborate index comprising physical, psychological, and social health. Much of what is discovered cannot be addressed by the medical care system. On the other hand, if we wish to assess the amount of need in our population, regardless of which system or organization can appropriately address it, then such an index is appropriate.

Estimation

The amount of need in a given population should be one of the determining factors in estimating resource requirements. We began this discussion with the statement that the medical care system exists to meet the need of the population. In order to meet that need, resources are required that must be translated into services.

As previously discussed, estimations of the number of physicians and beds are often derived from normative standards based entirely on population size. Lee and Jones (1933) demonstrated over 50 years ago that estimates of greater validity can be obtained by measuring need in population. With the more sophisticated methodologies now in the literature, a much more accurate estimate of not only the number but the type of resources required by any population is possible. Schonfeld, Heston, and Falk (1972) essentially replicated the Lee and Jones study to estimate that approximately half as many primary care physicians were available as were needed. Obviously, the more complex the instrument of measurement, the more costly it is to implement.

Priority-setting

Health care policy and resource allocation decisions are much more enlightened when based on some measure of need. The measurement instrument may be simple or complex, but in setting priorities, weighting takes on a very important role. It may be that certain disease conditions or certain age groups should be weighted differentially. Put another way, is the death of a 65-year-old person to receive the same weight as the death of a 2-year-old? Or, is the disability of a member of the workforce of more concern than the disability of a person of retirement age? In applying weights to the need measurement instrument, social, moral, and ethical values are built into the priority development process. The example of Great Britain discussed in Chapter 1 is a clear example of weighting workforce members more heavily than nonworkforce members.

In this text, measuring need is considered essential to recognizing the difference between total need in any given population and identifiable need. As discussed earlier, the only need that can be treated is identified need, and the amount and type of need identified is contingent on the measurement instrument adopted. It also bears repeating that not all identified need will necessarily be treated.

Discussion Questions

1. What are the implications of the level of need used in planning and establishing facilities for a medical care system?

2. What is meant by congruence, what are some possible determinants of the lack of congruence, and what are the implications for the medical care system?

3. Attempts to measure need in a population might be characterized as those relying on gross, readily available data and those that rely on more sophisticated, specifically gathered data. What are the advantages and disadvantages of these two need measurement types?

4. The reason for measuring need in a population can play an important role in how need is measured. What are the reasons for assessing need in a population and how do they relate to the metric used?

References

Arrow, K. "Uncertainty and the Welfare Economics of Medical Care." *American Economic Review* 53 (December 1963): 941–73.

Breslow, L. "A Quantitative Approach to the World Health Organization Definition of Health: Physical, Mental and Social Well-Being." *International Journal of Epidemiology* 1 (1972): 347–55.

Davies, A. R., and J. E. Ware, Jr. *Measuring Health Perception in the Health Insurance Experiment R-2711-HHS*. Santa Monica, CA: Rand Corporation, 1981.

Donabedian, A. *Aspects of Medical Care Administration: Specifying Requirements for Health Care*. Cambridge, MA: Harvard University Press for the Commonwealth Fund, 1973.

Eisen, M., C. A. Donald, J. E. Ware, Jr., and R. H. Brook. *Conceptualization and Measurement of Health for Children in the Health Insurance Study R-2313-HEW*. Santa Monica, CA: Rand Corporation, 1980.

Fanshell, S., and J. W. Bush. "A Health-Status Index and its Application to Health-Services Outcomes." *Operations Research* 18 (November–December 1970): 1021–66.

Gordon, J. E. *The Newer Epidemiology in Tomorrow's Horizon in Public Health*. New York: Public Health Association of New York City, 1950.

Katz, S., A. B. Ford, R. W. Moskowitz, B. A. Jackson, and M. W. Jaffe. "Studies of Illness in the Aged." *Journal of the American Medical Association* (21 September 1963): 914–19.

Koos, E. L. *The Health of Regionville*. New York: Columbia University Press, 1954.

Last, J. M. "The Iceberg; 'Completing the Clinical Picture' in General Practice." *Lancet* 2 (6 July 1963): 28–31.

Lee, R. I., and L. W. Jones. *The Fundamentals of Good Medical Care*. Chicago: The University of Chicago Press for the Committee on the Cost of Medical Care, 1933.

Mossey, J. M., and E. Shapiro. "Self-Rated Health: A Predictor of Mortality Among the Elderly." *American Journal of Public Health* 72 (August 1982): 800–7.

Patrick, D. L., J. W. Bush, and M. M. Chen. "Toward an Operational Definition of Health." *Journal of Health and Social Behavior* 14 (March 1973): 6–23.

Sanders, B. S. "Have Morbidity Surveys Been Oversold?" *American Journal of Public Health* 52 (October 1962): 1648–59.

Schonfeld, H. K., J. F. Heston, and I. Falk. "Numbers of Physicians Required for Primary Medical Care." *New England Journal of Medicine* 286 (16 March 1972): 571–76.

Somers, A. R., and H. M. Somers. *Health and Health Care.* Germantown, MD: Aspen Systems, 1977.

Stewart, A. L., J. E. Ware, Jr., and R. H. Brook. *Construction and Scoring of Aggregate Functional Status Measures, Volume I R-2551/1-HHS.* Santa Monica, CA: Rand Corporation, 1982.

Ware, J. E., Jr., R. H. Brook, A. R. Davies-Avery, K. N. Williams, A. L. Stewart, W. H. Rogers, C. A. Donald, and S. A. Johnston. *Conceptualization and Measurement of Health for Adults in the Health Insurance Study, Volume I: Model of Health and Methodology, R-1987/1-HEW.* Santa Monica, CA: Rand Corporation, 1980.

Winter, K. E., and C. A. Metzner. *Institutional Care for the Long-Term Patient.* Research Series No. 7. Ann Arbor: University of Michigan School of Public Health, Bureau of Public Health Economics, 1958.

Figure 5.1 Potency, Technology, and Quality—State of the Art

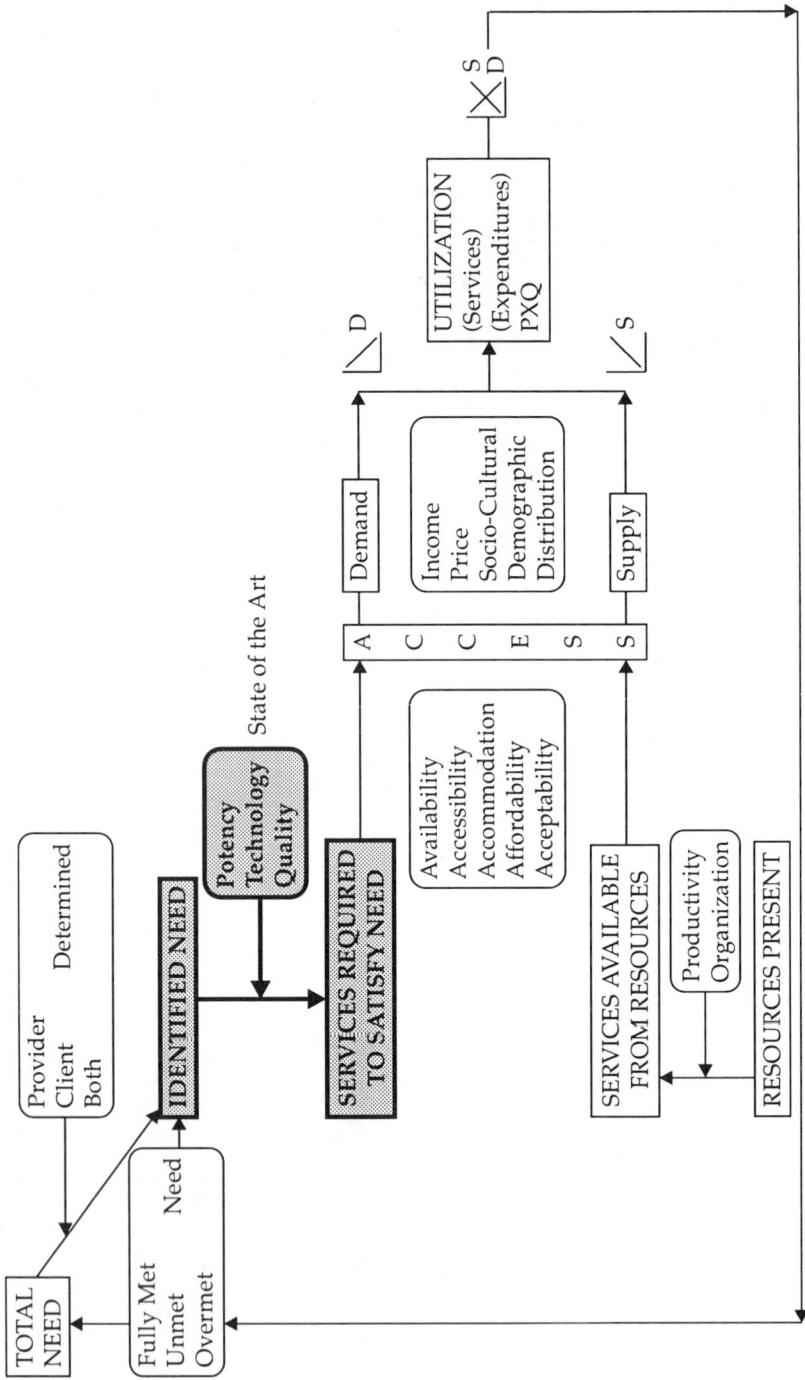

Chapter 5

The State of the Art

Having identified the need for medical care regardless of the definitional approach taken, let us think in terms of the number and type of medical care services that would be required to adequately address that need. In other words, if we were determined to treat all of this need in the population, what type and how many of each type of service would be required?

To answer this question, we must recognize that even though we are able to identify a need for care, the current state of the art in medicine may be such that there is no known care for certain needy conditions. Additionally, the number and type of services required to address a specific need may be one matter under ideal conditions but entirely different under something less than ideal conditions. If we have the highest quality of health care provision, the number and type of services required to treat a specific condition will be quite different from the number and type of services required to address that same need if the quality is anything less than the highest. With this in mind, the state of the art represents a set of modifying concepts that intervenes between *need* and *identified need* as exhibited in the shaded portion of the model shown opposite.

In this chapter, the intervening concepts of *potency* and *technology* are introduced, and their contribution to the mismatch between the medical care system and the type of care required is addressed. A discussion of the paradox of good medicine, which recognizes the tendency of the technology to discover disease outrunning the technology to cure disease, follows. Finally, the effect of the quality of the process of care on services required is discussed.

Potency and Technology

Posing two related questions to new students in the medical care field can be a most revealing exercise. The first of these questions is, What can be cured? and the second is, Can we cure, or just control?

Consider for a moment the leading causes of death for the Western world at the beginning of the century. Infectious diseases such as diphtheria, tuberculosis, pneumonia, and scarlet fever combined to cause the greatest number of deaths, with infant diarrhea ranking second. Until the 1940s, the dramatic reduction in death rates was not due in any way to the presence and use of medical care. Rather, the scourge of infectious disease was tamed by improved sanitation, nutrition, and housing and the discovery of antibiotics. Recall that the type of medical research that led to the discovery of antibiotics is not included in our definition of medical care; it would be classified as research and would be included in that very small component of national health care expenditures labeled as such. The relatively large-scale adoption of immunization programs during this time period also contributed greatly to the reduction in deaths due to infectious diseases.

The dramatic decrease in infant deaths due to diarrhea was primarily the result of improved water supplies and knowledge of and procedures for handling food. More successful birth-control techniques and their more widespread adoption also contributed to the drop in infant mortality.

Other nonmedical care factors were responsible for major improvements in the death rates. In summary, the reduction in mortality prior to the 1940s was due to: (1) environmental changes (water supply, sanitation, food handling); (2) immunization; (3) health education (food enrichment programs); and (4) social forces (e.g., safety awareness in the workplace).

The discovery in 1928 and the use in 1941 of penicillin ushered in the antibiotic era and further reduced death rates from infectious diseases.

The first half of the twentieth century witnessed a dramatic change in the leading causes of death. Heart disease, cancer, and stroke moved to the top of the list and remain there today, with 70 percent of all deaths attributed to these causes; in 1900, these three causes accounted for only 20 percent of the deaths. While some cause must always lead the list, it's a concern when the leading killers change so markedly. Not the least of the concerns arise from the fact that in addition to changing the research agenda, the medical care system must adapt to this new, and quite different threat. For example, the type of services required by a population where the leading cause of death is infectious disease is quite different from that required when the leading cause of death is degenerative disease. The magnitude of the problem engendered by this change is only apparent in recognizing that not only must the type of services provided be revised, but so must the education process of those who provide care.

Our current system might be described as one established with a heavy emphasis on cure. In other words, clients with symptoms enter the system where there is a diagnosis, intervention, and cure, and clients leave the system without symptoms. As is shown in Figure 5.2a, this type of medical care system can be likened to the proverbial "black box" wherein a miraculous intervention appears to take place. However, the system is now faced with clients for whom medical miracles cannot reverse the degenerative pathological process. For example, the damage inflicted by heart disease is long past by the time the patient reaches the sophisticated coronary care unit (CCU). Nevertheless, our emphasis and resources have been placed on the cure (in the CCU) rather than on the prevention.

In the medical care system portrayed in Figure 5.2, the left-hand side of the black box must be removed, allowing the system to reach back to attend to the clients before they reach the stage that would require entering the black box (Figure 5.2b). Of course, there will be those patients who must still enter the black box, which means that it must exist in the system.

It is somewhat of a cruel irony that many of the improvements to the system have resulted in the fact that it is now faced with an increasing number of clients with incurable diseases. This phenomenon (discussed in greater detail later) is recognized for

Figure 5.2   The Medical Care System and the "Miraculous Intervention"

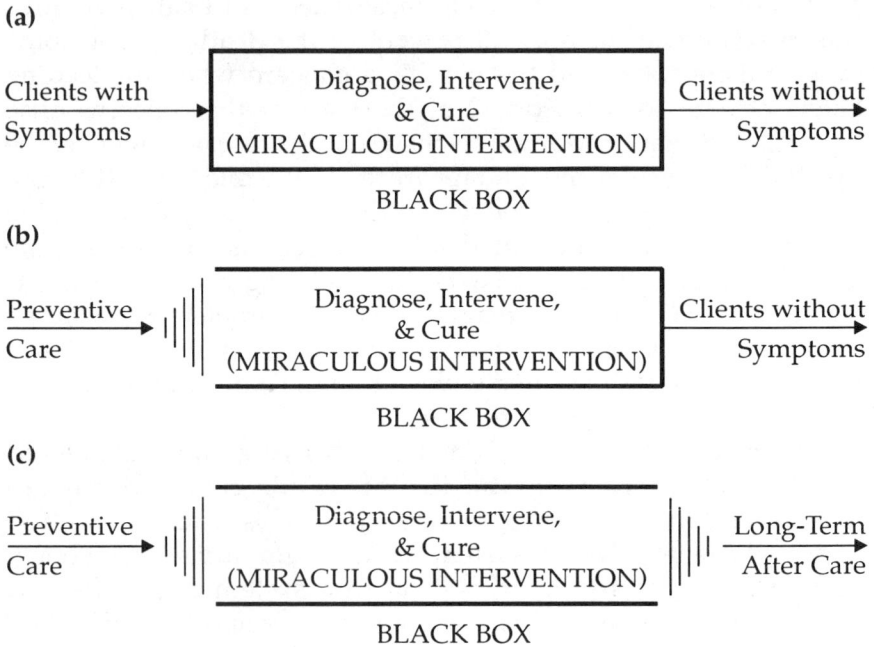

(a)

| Clients with Symptoms | → | Diagnose, Intervene, & Cure (MIRACULOUS INTERVENTION) | Clients without Symptoms → |

BLACK BOX

(b)

| Preventive Care | → | Diagnose, Intervene, & Cure (MIRACULOUS INTERVENTION) | Clients without Symptoms → |

BLACK BOX

(c)

| Preventive Care | → | Diagnose, Intervene, & Cure (MIRACULOUS INTERVENTION) | Long-Term After Care → |

BLACK BOX

its impact on this black box model of the medical care system. For example, for many cancer conditions we measure success in terms of survival rates over a given time period, which means that the clients can never actually leave the system and require care after the miraculous intervention. The right-hand side of the black box must now be removed, as shown in Figure 5.2c, allowing the system to provide continuing or long-term care to clients who were not cured by miraculous intervention.

Potency

The changing nature of disease has lead to an incongruence between the type of services required by the current disease pattern in the population and the type of services the system is capable of providing. In other words, we might postulate that the potency of the medical care system as a whole is marginal. This is not to say that for some particular disease or illness conditions, the system is not capable of providing exactly what is required. Indeed, the miraculous intervention can still work in some cases. The *potency* of the medical care system, however, refers to the ability of the system to ameliorate those conditions in the population that require care. Having discussed the difficulty of identifying the need for care, now it is apparent that the less potent the system is, the more services are required. For example, imagine a world where all medical care is maximally potent. In it, the services required to address the identified need in the population would be less than that required in our actual world where all services are not maximally potent.

Technology

Potency is, to a great extent, dependent on technology—that is, the ability to diagnose and treat clients is dependent on the skill of the providers and the technology available to them. (The skill of the provider will be addressed later in this chapter and in Chapter 6.) The impact of technology on the system is far-reaching. Its effect on the complexity, organization, and cost of the system will be discussed in Chapter 6, but now we will concern ourselves only with its effect on the service requirements.

The paradoxical effect

Having established the cruel irony of some of the medical care system improvements, we introduce the concept of "the paradoxical effect" of good medical care, which was described by Donabedian (1973). The *paradoxical* effect is a function of the three components—discovery, survival, and postponement.

The *discovery* effect refers to the ability to discover previously undetectable need for care and, therefore, a greater requirement of services. The increasing sophistication of medical technology has facilitated an ever-increasing microscopic and electronic probing of the human body and examination of its component parts. The result has been the discovery of ever-increasing need for care. In terms of what we discussed in Chapter 4, the clinical horizon is pushed continually downward.

A slight variation of the discovery effect might be referred to as the *exposure* effect, which occurs as medical care systems become more accessible, thereby encouraging more clients to use the system. With increased access, clients become more comfortable with the thought of seeing their physician, and increased exposure may lead the discovery of new disease or illness conditions. In fact, with the discovery effect the incidence and prevalence of disease increases, and it can be said that the better the medical care system, the greater the incidence and prevalence of disease (Donabedian 1973).

The *survival* effect refers to the capability of the medical care system to control disease but not cure it. For example, we now have the capability to control diabetes, but we do not have the capability to cure. Given this, more people survive with this condition, and as a result, more of the type of services specific to this survival are required. For conditions such as this, the incidence has not increased, but the prevalence has. Again, the better the medical care system, the greater the prevalence of disease conditions of this nature and, therefore, the greater the number of services required to address that need (Donabedian 1973).

The *postponement* effect refers to the capability of the medical care system to postpone death. In doing so, more individuals live long enough to become susceptible to the chronic conditions associated with growing old. This is not to suggest that those individuals who might fall into the category of "being kept alive" necessarily use more services than those who do not, rather that more services are required when more people are kept alive and kept alive longer (Donabedian 1973).

The paradoxical effect can be brought more sharply into focus by considering the following hypothetical scenario depicted in Figure 5.3.

Populations A and B are identical in terms of their living conditions and the availability of a myriad of social services; they are also identical in terms of their total infant mortality. The rate of infant deaths in population A, or during the first two or three days of life, is greater than that of population B. However, the 30-day infant mortality rate is greater in population B than it is in

Figure 5.3 Hypothetical Infant Mortality Rates and Medical Care Systems

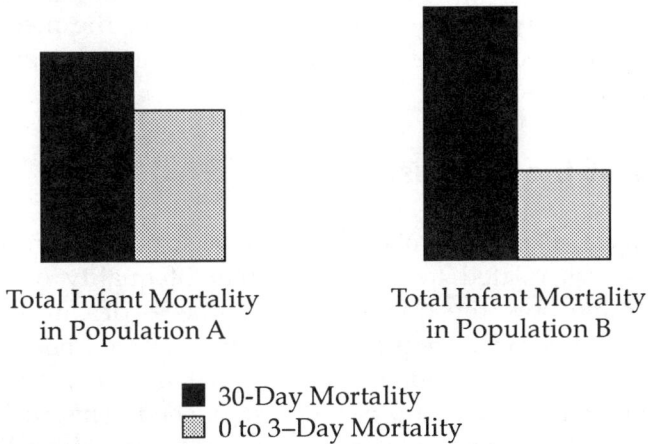

Total Infant Mortality   Total Infant Mortality
in Population A   in Population B

■ 30-Day Mortality
▨ 0 to 3–Day Mortality

population A. Which population is served by the "better" medical care system?

This is a very difficult question to answer. Indeed, no one could possibly answer the question empirically. From the advantage of dealing with the abstract rather than the concrete, we can call attention to the fact that better obstetrical care may very well lead to more infants being born alive, only to die several weeks later. For example, McManus and Newacheck (1989) cite a study of the Robert Wood Johnson Rural Infant Care Program (RICP), which found that RICP was associated with neonatal decline but not with postnatal mortality reduction.

To continue with this hypothetical scenario, we can speculate less cautiously that population B would require more medical care services. Figure 5.3 also helps us confront the ethical and moral dilemmas ever-present in any medical care system. Quite apart from the fact that the use of services would be greater, given the capabilities of the medical care system in population B, a contrived diagram such as this compels us to question whether population B is any better off. But how does one determine that or place a value on quality of life? Answering these questions is far beyond

the intent and scope of this text. Suffice it to say that the kind
of thinking that prevailed, for example in Great Britain when the
National Health Service (NHS) was under consideration, must be
seriously called into question. The debate included the belief that
as more people were able to take advantage of the medical care
system, more people would be "better off" and fewer services
would be required.

Quality of the Process of Care

In Chapter 1, Donabedian's paradigm of structure, process, and
outcomes was related to the assessment of quality of care. We
now examine how the quality of the process of care can affect
the number of services required to address a given need for care.
To do so, we must accept the notion that in many situations a
normative standard of care can be established. This means that,
for a given condition, a given number and type of medical care
services should be used if the highest quality of care is to be
delivered. For example, it is possible in some circumstances for
expert medical care providers to agree on a treatment protocol for
a given condition. That protocol can be translated into a strategy of
care or a set of specific number and type of services to be provided
to the typical patient of this type.

At this point in time, much has been written about practice guidelines. Although offered as recommendations rather than
standards, guidelines can be viewed as intervening similar to standards or protocol. Eddy (1990) refers to these guidelines as "practice policies" and suggests that four methodological approaches
exist:

1. Global subjective: is the subjective judgment of policymakers
2. Evidence-based: describes available evidence relative to a
   particular policy and subjectively compares benefits
3. Outcomes-based: ties the policy to available outcomes data
   on alternative practice methods
4. Preference-based: includes all of the above tasks and includes an assessment of patients' preferences.

In addition, the patient outcome research teams (PORTs), sponsored by the Agency for Health Care Policy and Research (AHCPR), have embarked on the task of identifying those practice strategies that appear to contribute to more desirable outcomes (American Academy of Orthopaedic Surgeons 1992).

It is important to recognize that not all patients fit the description of the typical patient. In fact, there are those providers who would have us believe that all their patients are atypical. Also, not all conditions currently lend themselves to agreement among practitioners as to what represents accepted treatment. In other words, for many diseases, illnesses, and conditions, providers vary a great deal in treatment patterns. Wennberg and his colleagues have suggested that this occurs mainly where there is uncertainty in the profession as to what represents the best treatment regimen (Wennberg, Barnes, and Zubkoff 1982). With the increasing activity in outcomes research, we should expect that more of the uncertainty will be removed and more standards will manifest themselves.

For our purposes in working with a conceptual model, we are not compelled to accept the conventions of the real world. One could argue that if, or when, the uncertainty is eliminated, a set of standards for all conditions will emerge. As that happens, our current practice will be revealed as "good" or "not so good" relative to those standards. That is to say, a standard exists for all disease or illness conditions, but in many cases that standard is not yet known. This means that for all patient types, we are currently providing a "good" or "not so good" set of medical care services, although in many cases we do not know what is good.

Let us return to the point of our discussion: If the quality of the process of care is poor, the medical care system is required to provide a different number or type of services than it would if the quality were good. We may not know if the quality is "good" or "poor" (in the case of uncertainty), and we may not be able to predict, even in cases of absolute certainty, whether poor quality will result in providing more, less, or simply a different type of service. We do know, however, that the number or type of services required when poor quality prevails will be *different* than the number or type when good quality prevails.

Let us now consider the hypothetical case of a physician with a client who has a disease condition for which there is no uncertainty regarding the treatment protocol. Let us assume that the client is an average patient and that the treatment strategy calls for three office visits over a six-day period with a penicillin shot every visit. If the physician provides four office visits and four shots, or four office visits and three shots, the physician is delivering poor quality medical care. Likewise, if the physician provides three office visits and three shots over a three-day period, he or she is delivering poor quality medical care. In fact, any combination other than three visits over a six-day period and one shot per visit represents poor quality medical care.

However, as essential as standards are to the assessment of quality, it is in no way suggested that they should or can be universal or temporally fixed. Since they emanate from the current state of the art, they will change as the state of the art changes. The state of the art—the accepted standards—may vary with time and with geographic location. In other words, standards should not represent some textbook or ideal set of protocols, rather the best of that which is available at a given point in time in a given place. This means that a regimen of treatment judged to have been of "good" quality in a third world country may very well be considered "poor" quality in a developed country. For example, in a country where magnetic resonance imaging (MRI) was not readily available, the diagnostic process for clients presenting low back pain could be judged to have been of high quality even though an MRI procedure was not performed. On the other hand, that same process could be judged to have been of poor quality in a country where MRI equipment was readily available.

Discussing the effect of the state of the art on the number and type of services required to address an identified need has to some extent contributed to one of the issues this text sought to clarify— to implicitly or explicitly convey the notion that providers in the traditional medical care system and the technology available to them determine the need, and therefore the services, required by the clients. To the extent possible, the term "provider" should be interpreted broadly enough to include any provider, traditional as well as nontraditional.

Seeking Care

To understand this interpretation, consider the process of seeking care, as shown in Figure 5.4.

From a state of well-being, the process of seeking care begins with the client feeling the need for care: the client recognizes the need for care but, at this point, is not aware of the type of care required. The client makes a choice to seek care, either by immediately entering the traditional medical care system (a) or by entering the nontraditional system (b).

Figure 5.4   The Process of Seeking Care

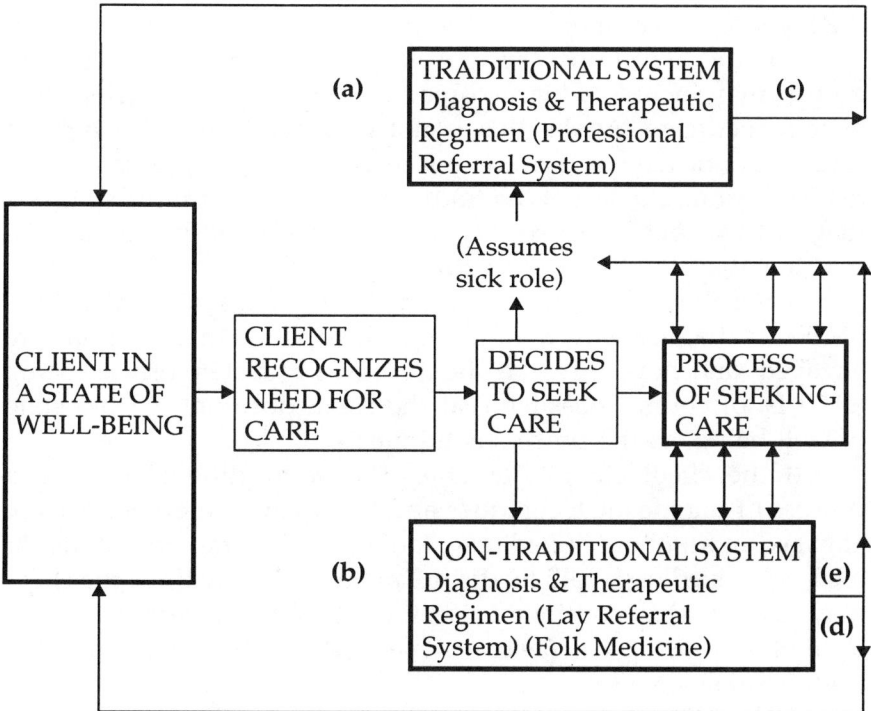

Note: Adapted from Avedis Donabedian, *Aspects of Medical Care Administration: Specifying Requirements for Health Care.* Reprinted by permission of Harvard University Press, Cambridge, MA. © 1973.

The nontraditional system ranges anywhere from consulting with family, friends, and clergy, to a well-established folk medicine or native medicine system—what might be called peripheral providers. In this context, peripheral providers would include legitimate providers of a specific service in the traditional system who give advice or care outside the realm of their accepted expertise. For example, many of us can recall asking the pharmacist to recommend a remedy for a particular ailment. We were using a traditional provider in the nontraditional system, and as such, that provider was then functioning as a peripheral provider in the lay referral system. This is not to suggest that the pharmacist does not have an important, legitimate role in the traditional system. It means that the extent to which the pharmacist is used in the manner described above is the extent to which they form part of the lay referral system.

The nontraditional system for certain ethnic or cultural groups may include a highly organized and sophisticated system of folk medicine. Again, this is not to suggest that this type of care does not have a legitimate foundation or a legitimate claim to be recognized a part of the traditional system. It simply suggests that, at this time in our society, it is considered to be outside the traditional system of medical care.

If the client chooses to enter the traditional system, the state-of-the-art diagnostic techniques and therapeutic interventions are engaged, and hopefully, the client returns to a state of well-being (c). It is, of course, possible that the client does not reach a state of well-being, so the process continues.

If the client chooses to enter the nontraditional system, a process of diagnostic techniques and therapeutic interventions are engaged in an unorganized (e.g., talk to mother; talk to friends) or well-organized (e.g., folk medicine) manner. At any time, the client may decide (1) to continue to seek nontraditional care, (2) that a state of well-being has been achieved (d), or (3) to move into the traditional system (e).

Although not illustrated in Figure 5.4, a client may choose to first enter the traditional system but then move into the nontraditional system to seek care, or a client may use both systems simultaneously.

In our society, a client has not assumed the sick role until that client has presented himself or herself to the traditional system. Only the traditional system can legitimize sickness in our current system. For example, a university instructor will not usually accept a note from a student's mother as proof that the student was sick and therefore unable to take an examination. The instructor would, of course, accept a note from a physician.

This discussion is not intended to either condemn or champion the nontraditional system and its lay referral individuals. Some countries fully embrace folk medicine as part of their traditional system, and numerous examples exist of traditional remedies sharing a common scientific base with folk remedies. However, there are some well-meaning people whose advice can be exceedingly dangerous, even deadly.

Rather, our purpose in introducing the concept of a traditional and a nontraditional system and the process of seeking care at this point is twofold. First, the extent to which clients with a legitimate need for care seek care in the nontraditional system is the extent to which that need will not be addressed by the traditional system. By accepting that need for care can be determined by the client, we understand that the number and type of services required to address the need in this case will not be required of the traditional system. In other words, the number and type of services required to address the identified need in the population by the traditional medical care system will vary with the extent to which clients seek care outside the traditional system. Second, if we accept that client-defined need is legitimate, then our definition of the traditional medical care system should be broadened to include some of the more legitimate lay referral individuals. As a postscript to this suggestion, the same requirements for standards acceptable to the experts in this field would apply if we wanted to measure quality.

Given the suggestion, for an identified need for care in any population, we can determine the number and type of services that would be required to address that need in an optimum manner. Before we change our focus in the model, we must fully acknowledge the medical care system as a "system" and not as a collection of independent, unrelated components. If something happens to change our definition of need, our ability to uncover need, our ability to cure, our ability to keep people alive, and our acceptance of what are currently considered to be nontraditional providers, then the number and type of services required by the population will change.

Next, we will explore what might be termed the supply side of the system.

Discussion Questions

1. The changing nature of disease has serious implications for the traditional medical care system. What are these implications?

2. How are potency and technology related to the paradoxical effect of good medical care?

3. How is the quality of the process of medical care related to the number and type of services required to treat a given amount of need in a population?

4. What is the lay referral system and what impact does it have on the number and type of services required of the traditional medical care system?

References

American Academy of Orthopaedic Surgeons. Committee on Outcome Studies. *Fundamentals of Outcome Research.* Parkridge, IL: The Academy, 1992.

Donabedian, A. *Aspects of Medical Care Administration: Specifying Requirements for Health Care.* Cambridge, MA: Harvard University Press for the Commonwealth Fund, 1973.

Eddy, D. M. "Practice Policies: Where Do They Come From?" *Journal of the American Medical Association* 263 (2 March 1990): 1265, 1269, 1272, 1275.

McManus, M. A., and P. W. Newacheck. "Rural Maternal, Child, and Adolescent Health." *Health Services Research* 23 (February 1989): 805–48.

Wennberg, J. E., B. A. Barnes, and M. Zubkoff. "Professional Uncertainty and the Problem of Supplier-Induced Demand." *Social Science and Medicine* 16 (1982): 811–23.

Figure 6.1 Services Available from Resources Present

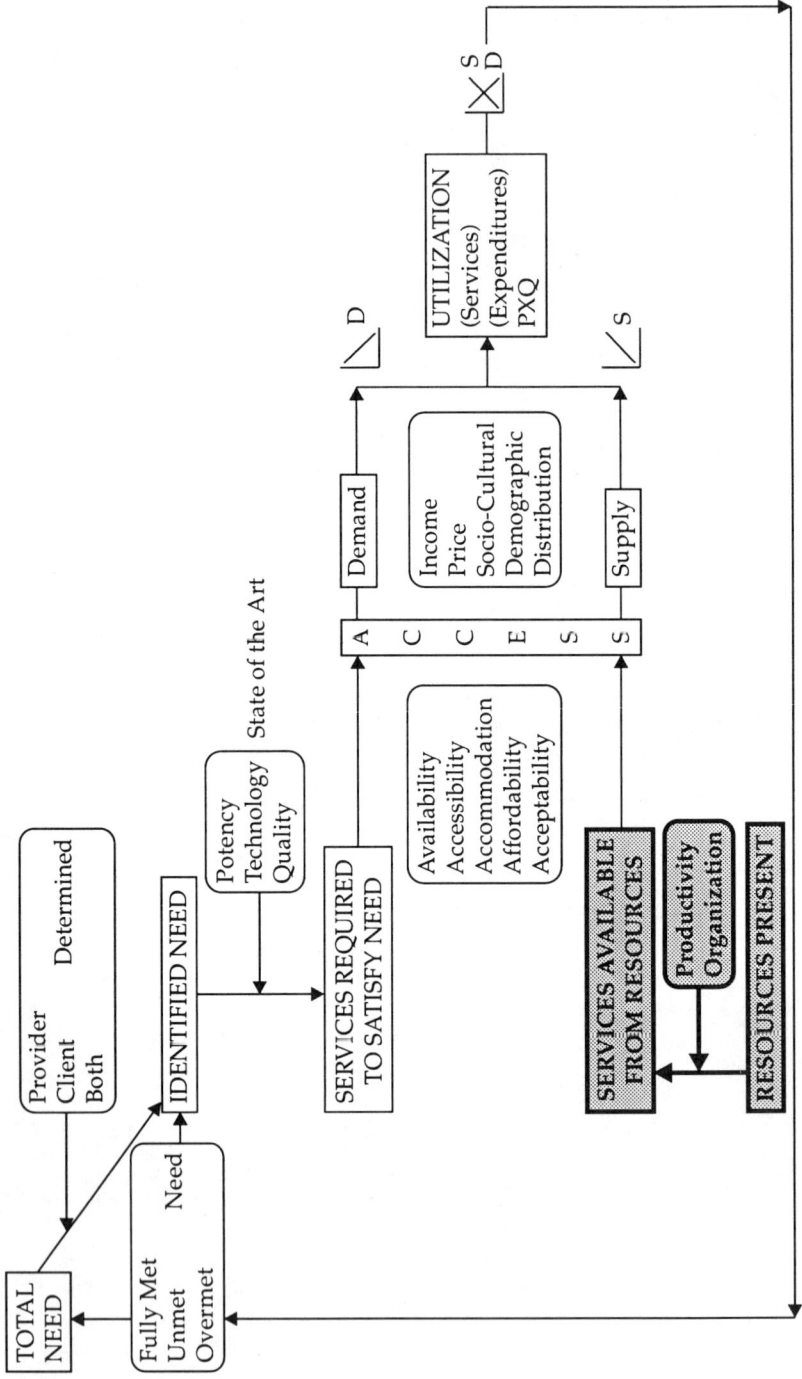

Chapter 6

Resources

For the next three chapters, our focus will be on the lower part of the conceptual model, as shown by the shading on the opposite page. This chapter discusses the importance of considering only those resources that are present, relevant, and active when determining the services available in the medical care system. The U.S. and Canadian systems are compared to illustrate the importance of using these qualifying factors and to highlight the necessity of using relative data rather than absolute numbers. Then the concept of assessing the quality of structure is reintroduced by briefly discussing its relationship to resources and costs.

All goods and services require certain inputs in their production, and medical care is no exception. An office visit, a hospital day, a physical therapy session, an x-ray, a laboratory test all require inputs that can be referred to as resources and can be categorized as either human or nonhuman resources.

Resources are allocated to the various sectors of the economy in different ways that to a great extent depend on the type of economy or system that prevails. It is beyond the scope of this text to discuss the various ways that resources can be allocated, but by referring to the discussion in Chapter 2, we revisit the idea that a purely competitive market system (libertarian) would allocate resources differently than a planned economy (egalitarian).

Regardless of the manner in which resources are allocated to the medical care system, a vital principle of economics prevails: resources are finite and demands for them are infinite. The importance of this, of course, is that resources devoted to one sector

Table 6.1 Actual and Adjusted Number of Resources Present: The United States and Canada

| | United States | | | Canada | | |
	(1) No.	(2) Resources/ Population	(3) Population/ Resources	(4) No.	(5) Resources/ Population	(6) Population/ Resources
Physicians	592,166	240/100,000	417/1	51,841	193/100,000	518/1
RNs	1,363,600	560/100,000	178/1	175,790	673/100,000	149/1
Dentists	149,000	60/100,000	1,667/1	14,177	54/100,000	1,865/1
Pharmacists	161,900	65/100,000	1,538/1	22,121	82/100,000	1,220/1
Beds	973,764	3.7/1,000	NA	167,010	6.2/1,000	NA

*Physicians, registered nurses (FTEs), dentists, pharmacists, and acute care hospital beds.
Sources: Roback, Randolph, and Seidman 1992. U.S. Department of Health and Human Services 1992; Health and Welfare Canada 1992.

of the economy cannot be devoted to another. So, the real cost to society of devoting certain resources to medical care is what it must give up in terms of other goods and services.

At the risk of oversimplifying the process and belaboring the point, human and nonhuman resources are allocated to the medical care sector by one means or another and form the basis for generating a specific number and type of service. As such, the number and type of resources that are present in the medical care system at one point in time must be considered. An important point to understand is that the mere presence of a resource in the medical care system is not a guarantee that the resource will be engaged in the production of a medical care service.

Present, Relative, and Active Stock

Rather than accept as a given that if a resource is identified as being present in the system it is engaged in producing services, think in terms of the present, relative, and active stock. *Present* should be interpreted as the actual number of resources available to the system. Knowing the number of resources without reference to the size of the population expected to use the services produced by those resources is not instructive. For example, knowing that population A has 2,000 physician resources available to it while population B has 8,000 physician resources available does not provide much useful information. In other words, by present we mean the actual number of resources available to a defined population. To bring this point more sharply into focus, consider the data in Table 6.1.

Columns 1 and 4 provide the number of physicians, registered nurses (RNs), dentists, pharmacists, and hospital beds in the United States and Canada. Those numbers indicate that in all five categories, the U.S. system has more resources available.

Columns 2 and 5 show the number of resources for every 100,000 persons in the population; columns 3 and 6 show the number of persons for every unit of resource. The numbers of resources have been adjusted by the size of the population in which they are present, which changes the picture. Whereas the United States has relatively more physicians and dentists, Canada has relatively more RNs, pharmacists, and hospital beds.

Tables 6.2 and 6.3 provide further evidence of the effect of adjusting resource numbers for population size within the U.S. (see Table 6.2) and Canadian (see Table 6.3) systems. Note that when the numbers are adjusted for population size, what might appear to be alarming differences are attenuated. It is also true that some perhaps surprising differences emerge, such as the greater number of RNs in Canada. This is not to suggest that using resource-to-population ratios represents the definitive word on resource availability. On the contrary, concerns over both the numerator and the denominator are central to the following discussion.

There is considerable attention paid to physician/population ratios, particularly in interregional comparisons. While it is much more appropriate to use these relative numbers rather than the unadjusted ones, there is a disquietening tendency to look to these ratios to provide standards. That is to say, we seem quite prepared to identify an area as overserved or underserved based on its physician/population or beds/population ratio. When we do this, we are in effect arguing that all populations are alike, all hospital beds are alike, and all physicians are alike, which, of course, is not the case.

Table 6.2 Variation in Physician Resource Present, United States, 1990

Area	No.	Physicians/ Population	Population/ Physicians
U.S. (whole)	592,166	240/100,000	417/1
New England	41,578	320/100,000	313/1
Mid-Atlantic	112,147	298/100,000	336/1
E. North Central	88,069	208/100,000	481/1
W. North Central	36,049	203/100,000	493/1
S. Atlantic	102,277	240/100,000	417/1
E. South Central	27,752	181/100,000	552/1
W. South Central	49,397	184/100,000	543/1
Mountain	27,894	208/100,000	481/1
Pacific	99,758	264/100,000	379/1

Sources: Roback, Randolph, and Seidman 1992; U.S. Department of Health and Human Services 1992.

Table 6.3   Variation in Physician Resource Present, Canada, 1991

Area	No.	Physicians/ Population	Population/ Physicians
Canada	52,863	187/100,000	535/1
Newfoundland	910	157/100,000	637/1
Prince Edward Island	175	135/100,000	742/1
Nova Scotia	1,760	191/100,000	523/1
New Brunswick	1,010	135/100,000	740/1
Quebec	14,241	200/100,000	500/1
Ontario	20,125	191/100,000	524/1
Manitoba	2,011	181/100,000	553/1
Saskatchewan	1,510	151/100,000	664/1
Alberta	4,351	166/100,000	602/1
British Columbia	6,682	195/100,000	512/1
Yukon	38	129/100,000	776/1
North West Territories	50	81/100,000	1,236/1

Source: Health and Welfare Canada 1993.

Instead, our concern should be for the type of bed or physician and the needs of the population. In other words, how many resources are present and capable of engaging in producing the type of service required by the population they serve. This is the *relative* component of the present, relative, and active stock concept. To illustrate: The presence of 150 pediatricians per 100,000 persons would be of very little benefit to a population, all of whose members are over the age of 60 years. Likewise, the presence of six beds per 1,000 persons would be of little use if those beds were pediatric beds.

The physician resource is as differentiated as the number of specialties and subspecialties that exist. In the interest of space and clarity, no attempt is made to examine the numbers in each specialty and subspecialty. Instead, we will consider one of the more important distinctions, that between the primary care physician and the specialist, as exhibited in Table 6.4.

While the United States had 235 physicians per 100,000 persons in 1990, it only had 27 general practitioners (GPs) and family practitioners (FPs) yet 208 specialists per 100,000 persons. The ratio

Table 6.4   Primary Care and Specialist Resource: The United
States and Canada, 1990

	United States		Canada	
	No.	Physicians/ Population	No.	Physicians/ Population
(A)				
GPs/FPs	68,428	27/100,000	27,334	102/100,000
Specialists	523,738	208/100,000	24,507	91/100,000
Ratio of GPs/FPs to specialists	1:8		1:0.9	
(B)				
Primary care*	162,680	65/100,000	27,334	102/100,000
Specialists	429,486	170/100,000	24,507	91/100,000
Ratio of primary care physicians to specialists	1:3		1:0.9	

*Because specialists in internal medicine serve as primary care physicians in
the United States, they are included in this number. In Canada, specialists in
internal medicine serve as consultants and not primary care providers.
    Sources: Roback, Randolph, and Seidman 1992; Health and Welfare Canada
1992.

of GPs and FPs to specialists in the United States is 1:8. In Canada,
the overall number of physicians is not that different from the
United States, 193 per 100,000 persons. Canada, however, has 102
GPs and FPs and 91 specialists per 100,000. The importance of
this for our discussion is that these two categories represent quite
different resources, capable of engaging in the production of quite
different services.

In the United States, specialists in internal medicine serve in
the capacity of primary care physician, which is not the case in
Canada. Perhaps the more important distinction is of that between
primary care providers and specialists. As can be seen in Table 6.4,
the ratio in the United States takes on a very different complexion
(1:3), yet the Canadian ratio remains the same (1:0.9).

The relativity of other resources is equally important. RNs,
for example, are as differentiated by their training—for example,

a trauma nurse versus a pediatric nurse. However, this does not suggest that any resource cannot be retrained to engage in the production of a different type of service. The time required to do this would vary with the type of resource, and since we are focusing on a snapshot, or one moment in time, the relative nature of the resource must be considered.

Hospitals, or to be more precise, hospital beds, should also be differentiated. While all of the beds in any system can be categorized in terms of the type of patients to whom they are dedicated, Tables 6.5 and 6.6 demonstrate a more general categorization.

The resource may be present or relative, but it may not be actively engaged in the production of services—it may not be *active.* The numbers of physicians and RNs provided in Table 6.1 are, in fact, active resources, but Table 6.7 shows how different active is from present.

Of course, there are many reasons why all RNs are not fully active in producing nursing services in the medical care system. The fact that over 400,000 trained RNs in the United States and 39,000 in Canada are not engaged in any way in the production of nursing services has serious implications for the training costs

Table 6.5 Hospital Resources in the U.S. System, 1992

	Nonfederal Short-Stay (< 30 days)		Long-Stay
Hospitals	5,105		447
Beds	901,396 (3.5/1,000)		

Bed Size	Hospitals	Beds	Percent Total Beds
<100	2,220	118,338	13
100–199	1,270	179,785	20
200–299	718	175,225	19
300–399	407	139,536	16
400–499	200	88,956	10
500+	290	199,556	22
	5,105	901,396	100

Source: American Hospital Association 1990.

Table 6.6   Hospital Resources in the Canadian System, 1989

	Public General	Public Special	Private	Federal
Hospitals	855	238	52	44
Beds	117,846	45,292	3,872	2,504
Total beds	169,514	6.3/1,000		

Bed Size	Hospitals	Beds	Percent Total Beds
1–49	499	12,075	7
50–99	214	15,035	9
100–199	188	25,485	15
200–299	106	25,835	15
300–499	118	44,218	26
500+	64	46,866	28

Source: Canadian Hospital Association 1993.

of this resource. Perhaps many of these RNs could not find employment in nursing. If so, then clearly too many RN resources are being allocated to the medical care sector, and the resource allocation dynamic is failing. It is also possible that jobs are available in geographic areas to which RNs are unwilling to relocate. If so, the resources cannot be considered present in those areas with job openings. A situation of this nature demands a policy addressing the maldistribution of resources, which also applies to the physician resource (see Tables 6.2 and 6.3). It would be impossible to examine all the policies that have attempted to address the maldistribution problem, but suffice it to say that most attempts to date have been relatively unsuccessful and the problem remains unsolved.

Why do many RNs work only on a part-time basis? It may be by choice, or it may be that full-time jobs are not available in the immediate area. Regardless, if all of those RNs listed as working part time in Table 6.7 were prepared or allowed to work an additional 25 percent of their time, 132,000 more RN resources in the United States and 18,000 more in Canada could be actively engaged.

It is not our purpose to consider the reasons why those trained as an RN, physician, or another type of medical care resource

Table 6.7 Present and Active RN Resources: United States and Canada, 1988

	United States			Canada		
	No.	*RNs/Population*	*Population/RNs*	*No.*	*RNs/Population*	*Population/RNs*
Present	2,033,032	824/100,000	121/1	249,827	957/100,000	104/1
Employed in nursing	1,627,035	660/100,000	151/1	210,000	807/100,000	124/1
Full-time*	1,099,576	446/100,000	224/1	120,951	463/100,000	216/1
Part-time*	526,489	NA	NA	71,120	NA	NA
FTEs	1,363,600	560/100,000	178/1	175,790	673/100,000	149/1

*Full- and part-time do not add to the number employed in nursing due to an "undetermined" number.
Sources: U.S. Department of Health and Human Services 1992; Health and Welfare Canada 1992.

are not fully engaged in producing services they are trained to produce. Our intention is to recognize that the appropriate number of resources readily available to produce services may be quite different from the numbers trained to do so. It also serves to focus attention on the fact that if the medical care system is perceived to be experiencing a shortage of any resource, the most appropriate and perhaps the most efficient way to resolve the situation is to persuade more of the trained resources to become fully engaged in producing services.

Having explored the resources available to produce services in the medical care system, we can now identify the number of each resource type and differentiate between the sometimes subtly different types. By understanding the concept of present, relative, and active stock, we can investigate the number and type of services that can be produced by the resources allocated to the medical care system.

The Quality of the Structure

It is at this point that the structure component of Donabedian's (1973) structure, process, and outcome quality assessment concept is analyzed. What is the quality of these resources? Are the facilities and personnel actively engaged in producing medical care services of the best quality, given the current state of the art?

The quality of facilities is assessed through the ongoing process of accreditation, as implemented by such bodies as the Joint Commission on Accreditation of Healthcare Organizations (JCAHO) in the United States and the Canadian Council on Health Facilities Accreditation (CCHFA). Each facility is examined periodically and evaluated against a set of criteria established to represent a given level of quality for a given type of facility. While there is some debate as to whether the criteria established by these organizations represents a sufficiently rigorous application of the components of quality, without doubt the accrediting process motivates quality on some level. A facility cannot afford to lose its accredited status.

The quality of personnel is generally assessed by the level of training received. Most professions in the health care field have established educational requirements for licensure or certification.

Securing the license is an indication of some implicit level of quality at which the individual is capable of working. Specialty boards also establish standards of quality incorporated in residency training programs, which are required of all those wishing to be designated a specialist. To be classified as such, the individual must complete the residency training program and successfully complete the examination set by the board. The various physician specialty training programs, for example, in the United States are accredited by the Accreditation Council for Graduate Medical Education (ACGME). This body serves as the coordinating body for all specialty education with input from each specialty's residency review committee. Each specialty board then examines graduates of these residency training programs and awards the diploma. This same function is performed in Canada by the Royal College of Physicians and Surgeons (RCPS) and the College of Family Physicians (CFP).

Contrary to the ongoing evaluation of the quality of facilities through the accrediting process, the quality of personnel is generally evaluated most rigorously at the beginning of the individual's practicing career. While more specialties are requiring reexamination for relicensure in the United States, it is by no means universal.

The purpose of this limited discussion of the various accrediting processes in the medical care field is to provide the context in which to place the quality assessment of structure. Using the type of information on the characteristics of the facility and personnel described, we can now assess the structural quality relative to a given patient type. For a given patient type, was the facility accredited by the appropriate authority and were the personnel duly recognized (license, diploma, fellowship, etc.) by the appropriate authority?

Technology and costs

Recall the technology/cost issue discussed in Chapter 5. As technology increases, criteria in the accrediting process will be revised to include the requirement of the new technological capability. New technology is also likely to spawn new subspecialties or, at the very least, new training programs for existing specialties.

These requirements are also likely to be included in accrediting criteria. As technology changes, structures and accrediting criteria will change to reflect the new technology. New technologies and new training programs represent more costly ways of delivering medical care. Although the care might be of higher quality, it is more costly. Therefore, increased technology or a higher quality structure is likely to lead to higher costs.

We can now see that resources may be present, they may be relevant, and they may even be active. The extent of their activity plays an important role in determining the actual number of services available to address the need in the population. This concept is discussed in the next chapter.

Discussion Questions

1. Physician/population ratios are often used as a measure of physician availability, particularly to define underserved and overserved areas. What are the problems with both the numerator and the denominator in these ratios?

2. What is the relationship between quality of structure, technology, and costs?

References

American Hospital Association. *Hospital Statistics, 1993–1994.* Chicago: The Association, 1993.

Canadian Hospital Association. *Guide to Canadian Health Care Facilities, 1993–1994.* Toronto: The Association, 1993.

Health and Welfare Canada. Health Information Division. *Health Personnel in Canada 1991.* Cat. H1-9/1-1991. Ottawa: Health and Welfare Canada, 1993.

Roback, G., L. Randolph, and B. Seidman. *Physician Characteristics and Distribution in the U.S., 1992.* Chicago: American Medical Association Department of Physician Data Services, 1992.

U.S. Department of Health and Human Services. Health Resources and Service Administration. *Health Personnel in the United States, Eighth Report to Congress 1991.* Pub. No. HRS-P-OD-92-1. Washington, DC: U.S. Department of Health and Human Services, Bureau of Health Professions, 1992.

Chapter 7

Productivity

The next step is to examine the process by which relevant resources are converted into services, which is not necessarily a one-for-one translation of resource to service. For example, if physician resources were increased by 10 percent, the number of services generated will not necessarily increase by 10 percent. This conversion of resources to services will be explored and referred to as *productivity*. Although the ardent economists may bristle at this use of the term, it is grammatically correct as a synonym for productiveness; it is the productiveness of the resources allocated to the medical sector.

This chapter will continue to focus on that part of the conceptual model preceding Chapter 6. The real costs of medical care services are determined here, and the economic concepts of *marginal product* and *economies of scale* are introduced. How these concepts influence determining the optimum combination of inputs in providing a medical care service (the best combination) and the optimum size of the service producing unit (the best size) are shown. Finally evidence of the difficulty of operationalizing these concepts is presented.

The manner in which the resources are combined and the size of the service-producing unit (e.g., physicians office or hospital) determine to a great extent the number of services that can be generated with a given number of resources. It is possible to generate more or fewer services with same number of resources, depending on how they are organized into the service-producing unit. An important implication of this concept is that if more services are produced with a given number of resources, the cost to produce each service (average cost) is less than would be if fewer services were produced with those same resources.

This is the point in our model where medical care costs, in the truest sense, are determined, thus, attempts to modify costs should also be focused here. The difference between *medical care costs* and medical care *expenditures* will be discussed in Chapter 10. For now, when most people use the term medical care costs, they generally are referring to medical care expenditures.

Again at the risk of raising the economists' hackles, we will oversimplify and draw on these economic principles to guide our discussion: *marginal product*, the *marginal rate of technical substitution*, and *economies of scale*[1] (see, for example, Ferguson and Maurice 1970). These somewhat threatening terms are not the preamble to an esoteric dissertation on the economics of medical care, but are introduced because of their utility at a level that can be more easily understood and, therefore, appreciated.

The Optimum Combination of Resources

If resources (inputs) are combined to produce services (output), is there an ideal combination and an ideal size of the service-producing unit? "Ideal" is used somewhat guardedly since it refers to the "least cost" combination and the "least cost" size. Before leaping in protest that least cost is not the only criterion for judging whether the combination or size is ideal, remember the caveat "all other things being equal." For our purposes, we assume that the quality of the service produced, by whatever combination of inputs or size of organization, remains the same. So if the same quality of service is produced for less cost, it is "ideal."

When considering the least cost combination of inputs, the marginal product (MP) of each resource is considered relative to the price it takes to engage that resource in generating services. The MP of any resource is the addition to output that results from the addition of a given amount of the resource. The price of the resource represents a cost to the production process. For example, the additional physician visits that result from another physician in the production of services is the MP of the physician input. The amount that must be paid to a physician to persuade him or her to engage in producing services represents the cost of those additional services. Knowing how much a resource can contribute and how much it will cost to generate each additional unit of output is a critical factor.

Additionally, knowing the MP of any input is also important in considering a possible change in the combination of inputs engaged in producing a given number and type of service. The MP indicates the number of services that would have to be replaced by another input if one input were removed and if it were required that total output be maintained. For example, if the physician resource at a given level of output has an MP of 200 visits per week and the nurse practitioner resource has a marginal product of 20 visits per week, 10 nurse practitioners would be required to replace one physician and maintain the same level of output. The ratio of the MPs of these two resources represents the rate at which they can be substituted for each other in the production of physician visits. This is known as the *marginal rate of technical substitution* (MRTS).

Obviously, the price one must pay to engage a physician in the production of services is quite different from the price one must pay to engage a nurse practitioner. The ratio of the price of these to inputs can then be compared to the ratio of their marginal products (the MRTS), and the point at which they coincide represents the least cost combination. If, in the example above, the physician input cost 10 times that of the nurse practitioner input, the combination of inputs engaged at that point represents the least cost combination.

A word of caution: the preceding discussion consciously presents a simple, neat scenario that might lead one to believe it is simple to employ. This is, of course, far from the truth, and there are many reasons for it, not the least of which is that although the price of inputs in the short run may not change, the MP of each input varies with the amount of the input currently engaged in the process (see Figure 7.1).

The fictitious data indicate the number of physician visits per week that can be produced by various combinations of physician and nurse practitioner resources. To measure the MP of nurse practitioners look across any row, holding the number of physician resources constant. In row 1, for example, the marginal product of

Figure 7.1 Resource Combination and Firm Size for Physician Visits

		Physician Visits per Week				
	5	840	860	850	845	825[a]
	4	730	770[c]	790	790[a]	770
Number of Physicians	3	610	620	670[a]	730[*]	700
	2	400[c]	420[a]	460	470[b]	480
	1	200[a]	220[b]	250	270	280
		1	2	3	4	5
		Number of Nurse Practitioners				

Note: Fictitious data were used to compile this table. See Berki 1973.

nurse practitioners is 20, 30, 20, and 10. In row 4, it is 40, 20, 0, and −20. Marginal product varies according to the number of nurse practitioners already engaged in the production process. Similarly, to measure the MP of the physician resource, look up any column, holding the number of nurse practitioners constant. In column 1, the MP of physicians is 200, 210, 120, and 110. In column 4, it is 200, 260, 60, and 55.

Consider the cell marked with an asterisk where 730 physician visits are produced. If one more nurse practitioner were added, the output would drop by 30 visits to 700, and if one more physician were added, output would increase by 60 visits to 790. On the other hand, if one nurse practitioner were removed, output would drop by 60 visits to 670, and if one physician were removed, output would drop by 260 visits to 470. At this point, the MP of each of these inputs has reached its maximum, 60 for the nurse practitioners and 260 for the physicians. The ratio of the two marginal products (MRTS) is 260:60 or 4.33. If we assume that the price of the physician input is $152,000 per year and the price of the nurse practitioner input is $35,000 per year, the ratio of input prices is 152:35 or 4.34. A combination of 4 nurse practitioners and 3 physicians represents the best combination of inputs at the existing price of inputs.

It can also be seen in Figure 7.1 that the same output of 730 visits per week could be achieved with 1 nurse practitioner and 4 physicians, which would cost $643,000, compared to $596,000 for the best combination of 4:3.

This phenomenon is significant because it can identify the best combination of resources in the production of any medical care service. It could be argued that, once this is known, no other combination could survive if the price of the service (the output) were in any way reflective of the cost to produce the service. In other words, the price of the service should be set to reflect the cost to produce the service using the best combination of resources, and all other combinations having higher costs would lose money for their producers.

This reasoning is fundamental to arguing for the use of other health care personnel where appropriate. For example, the right combination of midwives and obstetrical physicians could be determined for the service of child birth and perinatal mother and child care. Therefore, the best combination of resources for any service can be empirically determined and any other combination would be relatively more costly.

The Optimum Size of the Service-Producing Unit

Having examined the process whereby it is possible to determine the right combination of resources, we now consider the potential to determine the right size of the service-producing unit. As before, "right" in this context means the least cost—all other things being equal. The potential for making this determination can be explored by considering whether economies of scale exist. In other words, if the right combination of physicians and nurse practitioners in the production of physician visits is 4:3 (4 nurse practitioners to 3 physicians), is there any cost advantage in doubling or tripling the inputs in the same combination to 8:6 or 12:9? This proposition is akin to asking whether it is better to have three separate physician offices, all employing 4 nurse practitioners and 3 physicians, or to have one physician office employing 12 nurse practitioners and 9 physicians. If the one office produced more than 2,190 visits (three times that of the individual offices), then economies of scale exist, and it would be advantageous to insist on the larger units. If this were the case, the cost per visit would be reduced.

The data provided in Figure 7.1 are not extensive enough to provide a graphic presentation of this scenario, but they do allow us to examine the economies of scale concept. For example, consider the cells marked with the superscript letter *a*. All of these cells on the diagonal represent a 1:1 ratio of inputs. A ratio of 3:3 is no different from a ratio of 1:1 in terms of the combination of inputs; the only difference is that one is three times larger than the other. However, it's important to consider whether the number of visits increase by a multiple greater than the increase in inputs—is the number of visits produced with a 3:3 combination more than three times the number of visits produced with a 1:1 combination?

Using the data in Figure 7.1, the answer to this question is yes. A 1:1 combination generates 200 visits per week, and a 3:3 combination generates 670 visits per week, or 70 more visits than would be generated if there were no economies of scale. By carrying this examination a step further, a combination of 4:4 does not result in four times as many visits as a 1:1 combination (790 and 200). Nor does a 5:5 combination result in five times as many visits as a 1:1 combination (825 and 200). We can conclude then that if the best combination were 1:1, it is preferable to have service-producing units of the size 3:3 rather than 1:1. On the other hand, if the best combination were 2:2, it would be preferable to have two units of 2:2 (2 × 420 or 840 visits) than one unit of 4:4 (790 visits).

The cells in Figure 7.1 marked with the superscript letters *b* and *c* indicate the same ratio of inputs at different magnitudes of inputs. The cells marked with *b* reveal evidence of economies of scale, in that by doubling the inputs from 2:1 to 4:2, the number of visits more than doubles from 220 to 470. However, in the cells marked with *c*, *diseconomies* of scale exist. By doubling inputs from 1:2 to 2:4, the number of visits are less than doubled from 400 to 770.

The preceding discussion of marginal product and economies and the fictitious data used in Figure 7.1 draw heavily on the excellent work in this area by Berki (1973).

Understanding the concepts of marginal product and economies of scale is vital to understanding the argument of champions of health maintenance organizations. These two complex classic economics concepts will assist in facilitating comprehension of the

HMO movement in the United States and the health service organization and the comprehensive health organization movements in Canada. Throughout this text we have insisted on recognizing "all other things being equal," which means that for a given level of quality of care, larger organizations employing the right or ideal combination of inputs could conceivably provide services at less cost. It is always much simpler to discuss such important theoretical concepts in the abstract than to make use of them in the concrete. If economies of scale and *minimum optimum size* (MOS) are to become anything other than scientifically satisfying concepts, there must be consistent empirical evidence that such dynamics were present in the prevailing system. The search for this evidence has typically been conducted using cross-sectional analyses and has more often been directed at the acute and tertiary care facilities. In fact, a great deal of research effort in the late 1960s and early 1970s was devoted to attempts to identify the optimal bed size of hospitals of different types. These attempts produced a set of very ambiguous results ranging from 160 to 2,580 beds. Table 7.1 shows some of the results of these investigations (Long et al. 1985).

A testament to the difficulty in obtaining consistent empirical evidence of economies of scale lies surely in the list of leading scholars identified in Table 7.1. Although, 20 years later, we have more weapons in our research armamentarium, the critical concerns regarding cross-sectional research—an accurate measure of size, a clear and consistent definition of output, and an accurately specified model—still remain. The difficulties associated with these concerns may explain the lack of research activity in this area since the mid-1970s.

Productiveness can be extended to inputs other than the human one. For example, at any one point in time, it may be found that hospital beds are occupied or unoccupied. Unoccupied beds are what Donabedian (1973) refers to as "manifest reserve." This is analogous to the nonactive personnel, discussed regarding present, relative, and active stock in Chapter 6. Since a hospital rarely plans to operate at 100 percent occupancy, it is possible that at least some of the unoccupied beds are planned. To the extent that the manifest reserve was planned, one might consider it appropriate for the beds to be empty. However, consistently low occupancy

Table 7.1 Summary of Economies of Scale Research Findings

Investigator	Economies of Scale (EOS) Present and/or Minimum Optimum Size (MOS)
Cohen (1967)	MOS 160–170 beds
Cohen (1970)	EOS present, no estimate of MOS
Carr and Feldstein (1967)	MOS 350 beds
Berry (1974)	MOS 838 beds all hospitals
	429 beds voluntary hospitals
	1,274 beds government hospitals
	283 beds proprietary hospitals
Ingbar and Taylor (1968)	EOS present beyond 150–200 beds
M. Feldstein (1968)	MOS 2,580 beds
	310 beds
	250–300 beds
	900 beds
	(depending on the model used)
Ro (1968)	MOS 794 beds

Source: Long et al. 1985.

rates are surely indicative of the nonproductiveness of the bed input (Donabedian 1973).

Unoccupied beds are not the only concern when considering the productiveness of beds. It is important to know whether the occupied beds are appropriately occupied: even if the occupant of the hospital bed is in need of some medical care, is it necessary for that patient to be in hospital occupying a bed? Donabedian (1973) refers to this as "latent reserve."

At this point, the reader should be comfortable with the idea that a given amount of resources could generate differing numbers of services, depending on how they are combined in the production process. It is also important to keep in mind the major thesis of this work—the total system concept, or understanding that the productivity concept is not enough and that its place in the system must be recognized. It is at this point that costs are determined and any change in productivity can reverberate through the system, affecting all of the other components of the system—those we have already examined and those we have yet to examine.

Discussion Questions

1. Marginal product, productivity, and economies of scale are important economic concepts in determining the most efficient method of producing medical care services. How do these concepts relate to the combination of inputs that should be used and the size of the service-producing units?

2. Why has it been so difficult to determine the minimum optimum size of a hospital?

Note

1. Any introductory economics text will discuss these principles in detail.

References

Berki, S. E. "The Economics of New Types of Health Personnel." In *Proceedings from the Macy Conference on Intermediate Level Health Personnel in the Delivery of Direct Health Service*, edited by V. W. Lippard and E. F. Purcell. New York: The Josiah Macy Foundation, 1973.

Berry, R. E., Jr. "Cost and Efficiency in the Production of Hospital Services." *Milbank Memorial Fund Quarterly, Health and Society* 52 (1974): 291–313.

Carr, W. J., and P. J. Feldstein. "The Relationship of Cost to Hospital Size." *Inquiry* 4 (1967): 45–65.

Cohen, H. A. "Hospital Cost Curves with Emphasis on Measuring Patient Care Output." In *Empirical Studies in Health Economics*, edited by H. E. Klarman, 279–93. Baltimore, MD: Johns Hopkins University Press, 1970.

————. "Variations in Cost among Hospitals of Different Sizes." *Southern Economics Journal* 33 (1967): 335–66.

Donabedian, A. *Aspects of Medical Care Administration: Specifying Requirements for Health Care.* Cambridge, MA: Harvard University Press for The Commonwealth Fund, 1973.

Feldstein, M. S. *Economic Analysis for Health Service Efficiency.* Chicago: Markham Publishing Company, 1968.

Ferguson, C. E., and S. C. Maurice. *Economic Analysis.* Homewood, IL: Richard D. Irwin Inc., 1970.

Ingbar, M. L., and L. D. Taylor. *Hospital Costs in Massachusetts.* Cambridge, MA: Harvard University Press, 1968.

Long, M. J., R. P. Ament, J. Dreachslin, and E. J. Kobrinski. "A Reconsideration of Economies of Scale in the Health Care Field." *Health Policy* 5 (1985): 25–44.

Ro, K. K. "Determinants of Hospital Costs." *Yale Economic Essays*. New Haven, CT: Yale University Press, 1968.

Chapter **8**

The Organization of Resources

Having discussed the best combination and best size in relation to service-producing units, we now consider how, in fact, the subsystems within the medical system are organized. We continue to focus on that part of the conceptual model shown at the beginning of Chapter 6, and in particular on organization.

This chapter will first briefly consider what we have come to think of as the traditional system, and then some of the emerging trends that represent changes to that system will be discussed. Managed care from the perspective of patient- and system-level management will be examined. At the patient level we consider case management, particularly the gatekeeper model, and at the system level we discuss several forms of organization that include health maintenance organizations (HMOs) and preferred provider organizations (PPOs) in the United States and health service organizations (HSOs) and comprehensive health organizations (CHOs) in Canada. This will lead naturally into a look at regionalization.

The Traditional System

First let us examine the subsystem of the physician practitioner. To do so, it is necessary to explore several different components of the subsystem—the type of practice, the type of practitioner, the method of practitioner reimbursement, and the method by which the client pays for the service. If each of these is a continuum, the evolving practitioner system can be examined more readily, as illustrated in Figure 8.1.

Although it may appear that the position on one continuum may dictate the position on another of the continuums, this is not necessarily the case. For example, one might be tempted to argue that if a physician is a solo practitioner, he or she would not be an employee and would not be salaried. This, of course, is not always true since some physicians are employed by individuals and companies and paid a salary or a contracted amount. Or, the method by which the practitioner is reimbursed does not necessarily determine the manner by which the client pays for the service. Further, if a physician is working in a group setting and the group is reimbursed for physician services by fee-for-service, the individual physician may be reimbursed in any of the possible ways on the continuum—a group may be reimbursed for services rendered by fee-for-service, but individual physicians within the group may be paid a salary.

Figure 8.1 shows at the extremes that a physician may have a solo practice or work in an organized group; the continuum implies all possible variations within this range. Regardless of whether the physician is in solo or group practice, he or she may be an entrepreneur or an employee, or any variation within the continuum. Reimbursement may be made by fee-for-service, or by any one of a range of possibilities that would include capitation and, at the extreme, salary.

The mode of client payment is included in this model of organization because of its substantial potential to influence the

Figure 8.1   Practitioner Organization

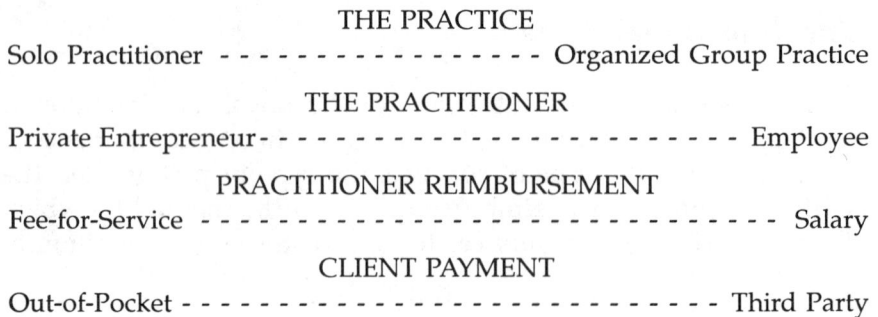

THE PRACTICE
Solo Practitioner - - - - - - - - - - - - - - - - - Organized Group Practice

THE PRACTITIONER
Private Entrepreneur - Employee

PRACTITIONER REIMBURSEMENT
Fee-for-Service - Salary

CLIENT PAYMENT
Out-of-Pocket - Third Party

system. As discussed above, these components must be viewed as separate and distinct, yet, the power of the purchaser (monopsony power) cannot be ignored. The extremes of the continuum of client payment are out-of-pocket and third party payer. The extent to which total payment to physicians is aggregated within a few third party payers is the extent to which these purchasers can exert pressure. The pressure may not come in the form of a dictate as to how physicians should be organized, but the pressure to reduce or constrain total expenditures may persuade physicians to consider alternative ways of practicing. A third party can be a public or private health insurer or welfare or charity arrangement.

From this limited discussion, we can describe the traditional physician subsystem (at least until the 1960s) as one comprising solo practitioners who were private entrepreneurs paid fee-for-service with clients paying out-of-pocket. In the not so distant past, the "fee" in fee-for-service often took the form of such things as chickens, potatoes, and other goods and services. This method may have been the original relative value scale.

An important feature of this physician subsystem is the exclusion of the hospital subsystem. In fact, the hospital subsystem remained completely separate with independent facilities owned and operated by a variety of public and private authorities. Community hospitals that were investor-owned or not-for-profit government- or nongovernment-owned operated independently, serving as what Pauly (1980) called the "doctor's workshop." The hospital afforded certain physician privileges and provided the equipment and support staff that allowed them to do their work.

Over the years, the traditional mode of physician practice has changed considerably. Most physicians now practice in some form of group arrangement, and most clients pay for service through a third party. However, the majority of physicians remain private entrepreneurs with reimbursement still predominantly fee-for-service. Until very recently, changes to the traditional system did not integrate the hospital subsystem in which the complete episode of care was addressed. In addition, until recently, these changes in physician practice were not generally the result of determining what the "best" combination of resources and the "best" size of service producing unit was. It was more the result of idiosyncratic cooperative efforts.

In Chapter 7 we suggested that in a competitive market, a service-producing unit that did not conform to the "best" combination and the "best" size could not continue to exist. The reimbursement formulas being implemented by many third party payers involved in the medical care field are based in some way, albeit loose, on value for money. That is to say, more third parties, perceiving themselves to be the purchaser, are demanding accountability by setting market prices. This is done in a variety of ways that includes setting prices based on resources used during the treatment process—for example, the resource based relative value scale (RBRVS) (Hsiao et al. 1988) and diagnosis-related groups (DRGs) in the prospective payment system (PPS) (Fetter et al. 1980). It might be said that third parties are substituting for the market forces that exist in a competitive market system. It should be pointed out, however, that the extent to which reimbursement in the physician subsystem and the hospital subsystem remain separate and distinct, is the extent to which the two systems will remain disconnected.

Managed Care Systems

Attempts have been made to integrate the physician and the hospital subsystems into what might be described generically as alternative delivery systems (ADS), which because they involve some form of managed care, have become known as managed care systems. To better facilitate our discussion, we distinguish between (1) managing care for an individual patient and (2) managing the delivery system. In the first category, we include what is known as case management, and in the second, all variations on the HMO and PPO themes, including the Canadian CHOs and HSOs. To identify certain underlying requisites for any managed care or alternative delivery system, our discussion will be limited to the most generic of these organization types.

Case management

Case management can take several forms; three models have particularly been identified by Merrill (1985)—medical, sociomedical, and social. These models differ in the extent to which they include social and medical services, which of course dictates the type of professional used as the case manager.

Given the theme of this book, the medical model will direct our discussion. Hurley and Fennell (1990) describe a case manager as one who takes responsibility for providing or authorizing a specified set of services.

Case management has been applied to *specific components* of care such as inpatient care, outpatient care, long-term care, and home care, and it has been applied to the *entire episode* of care. When applied at the single component level, the care that is given during that specific component of the entire episode is carefully planned and monitored. No attempt is made to manage the total episode of care in which the client may have been previously, or will be eventually, involved. A good example of this is in acute care facilities where the treatment provided within the facility is carefully monitored or managed up to the point of discharge planning. Typically, this type of case management will involve protocols and standards of care, as discussed in Chapter 5.

A more ideal case management system would include management of the client's case throughout the three potential levels of care—preadmission, inpatient, and postdischarge. Although this could conceivably exclude vital services for some clients, it identifies the spectrum of care that applies to the majority of patients in the medical care system—that is, it identifies the entire episode of care for the majority of clients. In these cases, the *gatekeeper model* is used.

Gatekeeper model

In the gatekeeper model, a primary care physician is the single point of entry into the medical care system and must approve all care. Typically, the physician receives a fee for acting as the gatekeeper and a capitation amount to provide all primary care to the client. Figure 8.2 illustrates a generic gatekeeper model.

All potential clients (enrollees) participating in the managed care arrangement must sign up with a specific primary care physician. It is absolutely essential to the viability of the program that the population served be unequivocally identifiable with a specific primary care physician. In the institutional case management

Figure 8.2   The Gatekeeper Model

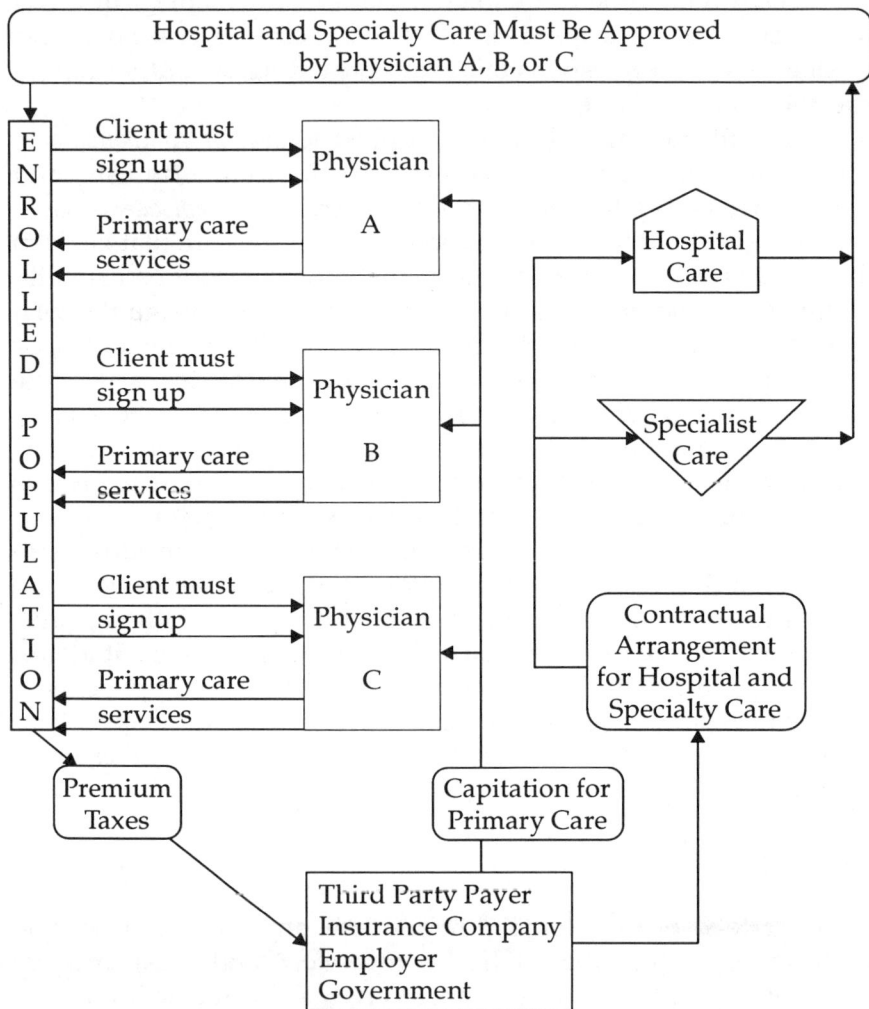

model, on the other hand, the patient is of course captive and therefore readily identifiable with a specific provider.

Enrollees either pay a premium or it is paid for them by a third party who negotiates a capitation rate with the primary care providers. For the established capitation amount, the primary care physician must provide all of the primary care required by all of those enrollees on the physician's list. Only the primary care services in the agreed upon benefit package are provided. In addition to this, the primary care physician must approve all other care before it can be given. Emergency care is, of course, exempt from this requirement, but all other specialist and inpatient care must first receive approval from the gatekeeper. The key is that the third party will not pay for care that is not approved by the primary care gatekeeper, although the arrangements for paying the hospital and specialist remain quite separate from the capitation amount paid to the primary care physician.

The importance of having a population that is unequivocally identified with a specific primary care physician is quite obvious. When called by a specialist or hospital to approve treatment for a particular patient, the physician knows the patient and can provide information that can contribute to a more informed decision regarding the treatment regimen. It also prevents the potential for duplicated (unnecessary) services that could result when clients move from one primary care physician to another.

However, note that in the Canadian system, clients cannot consult with a specialist without being referred by a primary care physician. The client is not required to be unequivocally assigned to one particular primary care physician. Therefore, in the Canadian system there is de facto approval of nonprimary care so a gatekeeping model prevails. The client can, nevertheless, see different primary care physicians in search of a sympathetic one, and the third party (provincial government) does not require evidence of approval before paying for nonprimary care. This assessment of the Canadian system is not intended to imply that the issue of primary care physicians sanctioning specialist care has been resolved in the U.S. gatekeeper model. This is far from the case and is, in fact, one of the bigger obstacles to a successful gatekeeper system.

An interesting variation on the gatekeeper theme, the SAFECO experiment was unsuccessful in the 1970s (Martin, Ehreth, and Geving 1985): Rather than paying a capitation amount for primary care only, the third party paid the primary care physician an amount intended to cover all care from all providers. In SAFECO, the primary care physician became the "purchaser" of all care rather than just the "approver" of care. As is the case with all capitation systems, the primary care physician received a per capita amount estimated to sufficiently cover all included care. If the enrollee received no care, the gatekeeper still received the full capitation amount. If, on the other hand, the enrollee received $10,000 worth of care and the capitation amount was $1,000, the gatekeeper lost money for that particular patient.

It isn't much of an intellectual stretch to argue that the primary care physician, as the purchaser of care, became the consumer of care in the SAFECO experiment. As such, he or she is a more knowledgeable consumer than the usual client and is more likely to conform to the classic economists' perception of the knowledgeable consumer. The underlying concern in all capitation systems is that the built-in incentive is for the physician to underserve the enrolled population. The failure of the SAFECO experiment was due in large part to the failure of the physicians involved to come to terms with the idea of a primary care physician determining, to some degree, how specialists would practice.

In both the institutional case management and the gatekeeper models of managed care, the goal is provision of appropriate and necessary care at a reasonable price. Although the decisions made in such systems are not usually predicated on the scientific process described in Chapter 7, the underlying dynamics implicitly draw on those concepts.

System management

As a framework to facilitate our discussion of the various attempts to manage the system or episode of care, we use the several variations of the HMO model in the U.S. and Canadian systems. They might be viewed as variations in an attempt to manage the amount and type of care provided to a given population, so with this in mind, our discussion is confined to the underlying principles of the generic models examined.

When HMOs first appeared, three models gained some acceptance—staff, group, and independent practitioner association (IPA). Because the group and IPA models are so similar in their underlying concept of system control, our discussion can be limited to the staff and the IPA/group models.

Staff-model HMO

In an ideal staff-model HMO, the organization employs physicians and other health care workers and owns the hospitals. All workers, including physicians, are salaried employees, and the hospitals in the system plan and justify their operating budgets. The primary difference between this type of organized system and most others is that all health care providers rely completely on the organization for their livelihood, and the facilities belong to the organization. As such, a staff-model HMO very much resembles organizations in other sectors of the economy. For example, at a General Motors plant, the personnel are employees and the facilities belong to General Motors. In these types of organizations, management control is characterized as tight or strong. Figure 8.3 presents the staff-model HMO; the bold line surrounding the total system illustrates the extent to which the total system is under control.

Detractors of the staff model argue that the client's choice of physician is severely restricted, which compromises the quality of care. Perhaps the greatest criticism, though, is that, as with all organizations operating on a predetermined, fixed budget, there is an implicit incentive to underserve the client. In all studies comparing

Figure 8.3   Staff-Model HMO

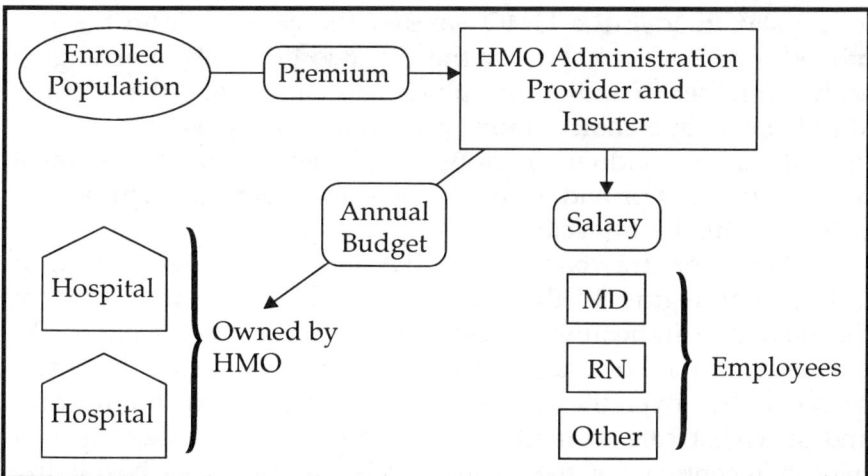

HMO populations with populations receiving their care in the conventional manner, the HMO populations use less care (Luft 1978). This is due primarily to the fact that HMO clients use less inpatient care, which is not attributable to an HMO's success at keeping its population healthy, but the result of the rigorous application of protocols and standards of care, or the amount of control. The work of Luft (1978) has cautioned that in restricting the use of services, necessary care as well as unnecessary care, is restricted. In all the studies that have successfully controlled for population characteristic differences, no discernable differences in health outcomes have been uncovered between a population receiving its care through an HMO and a population receiving its care in the conventional manner. For example, see Sloss et al. 1987 and Ware et al. 1986.

IPA/group-model HMO

The ideal IPA-model HMO features the organization arranging for the client to receive primary care from an individual or group of physicians in return for the capitation payment. If a client requires inpatient or specialty care, the primary care physicians simply refer the client or hospitalize him or her according to usual practice procedures. The HMO then reimburses the specialist or hospital according to a separate arrangement from a separate fund.

A major distinction between the staff and IPA models is that in the staff model, the HMO *provides* the care while in the IPA model, the HMO *arranges* for the client to get care. In arranging with a number of individual physicians or groups, the client is afforded a greater choice among physicians. However, once signed up with an individual or group of physicians, the client must remain with that provider for at least as long as the benefit period, which is usually one year.

The major drawback to the IPA model is in its control, or lack thereof. Figure 8.4 illustrates the IPA-model HMO. Note that the bold line indicating control does not encompass either the physician or the hospital, demonstrating that the HMO has little, or no control over the total system. Since payment for hospital and specialist care is made from a separate fund, there is a financial incentive for the primary care physician to hospitalize patients inappropriately. The HMO attempts to introduce a dis-incentive, or controls, by instituting a "hold back fund," which places the physician or group of physicians at risk for the amount of the "hold back fund," typically 20 percent of the total capitation amount. As a result, studies comparing service use by IPA- and staff-model HMO enrollees found that the staff-model clients used fewer services (Luft 1978).

Preferred provider organizations

Although usually discussed under managed systems, preferred provider organizations (PPO) are not so much an organization as

Figure 8.4 IPA (or Group) Model HMO

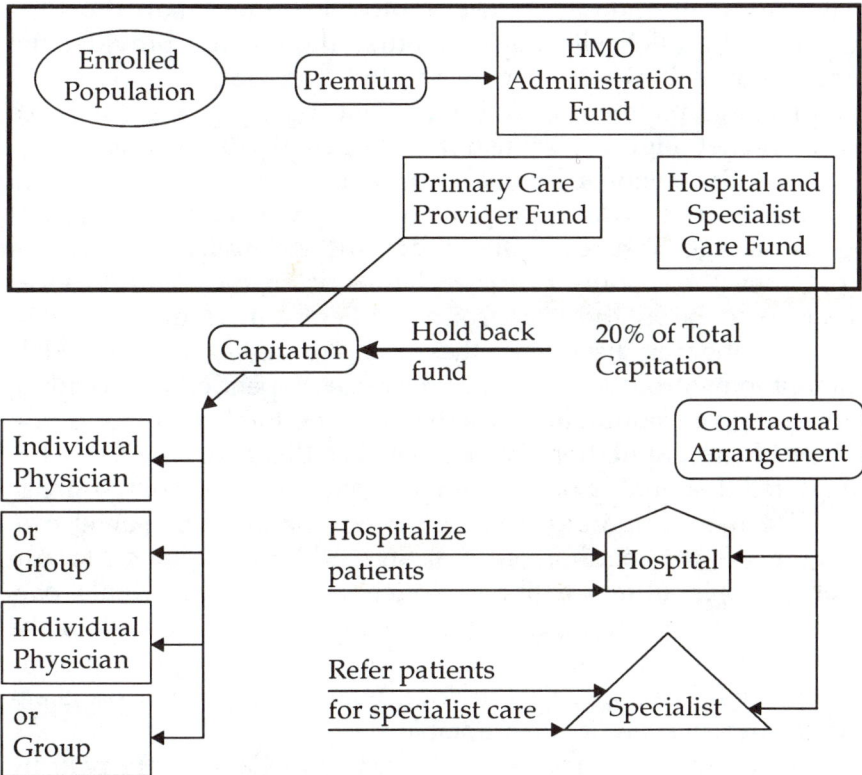

a brokering arrangement between providers and purchasers. As such, there are a multitude of possible arrangements that give rise to the often-quoted observation, "when you've seen one PPO, you've seen one PPO."

Acknowledging that purchasers are generally an employer, an insurance carrier, or some other third party such as government, the purpose of the PPO, then, is to arrange for the delivery of specified health care services at a negotiated price to an identifiable group of subscribers or clients. The negotiated price is a discount that facilitates a reduced premium rate for the enrollees, and guarantees the provider a volume of business.

In addition to an identifiable group of clients, the reduced premium, and the discounted price, a PPO is characterized by a defined and restricted provider panel. Controls must be implemented to prevent the clients from seeking care outside the system. This is achieved through the use of a "swing option," which means that if a client chooses to use a provider other than the PPO provider, the PPO will only reimburse the outside provider the same amount it would pay to the PPO provider. If this is not acceptable as payment in full, the client must pay the difference out-of-pocket. Figure 8.5 illustrates the generic PPO model.

This discussion of some generic managed care models in the United States was appropriately cursory, yet several relevant points emerge. Whatever the model, the emphasis is clearly on controlling the amount of expenditures on medical care services for a given population or group of clients. In terms consistent with this ongoing discussion, these types of managed care models attempt to control the amount of resources expended in providing care to a given population whether it is the total population or a subset of the population. Remember that this discussion has not suggested that quality be reduced to successfully control resources.

The most important element of any of these managed care programs is the requirement that an enrolled population be unequivocally identified with a provider. To many individuals, particularly the libertarian, the requirement that all members of the population or subset of the population, at any one point in time identify with one specific provider, is an infringement on client choice, and as such, is unacceptable.

In contrast, physicians and hospitals in Canada are paid by the provincial government, so in effect, the potential for a very

Figure 8.5 Preferred Provider Organization

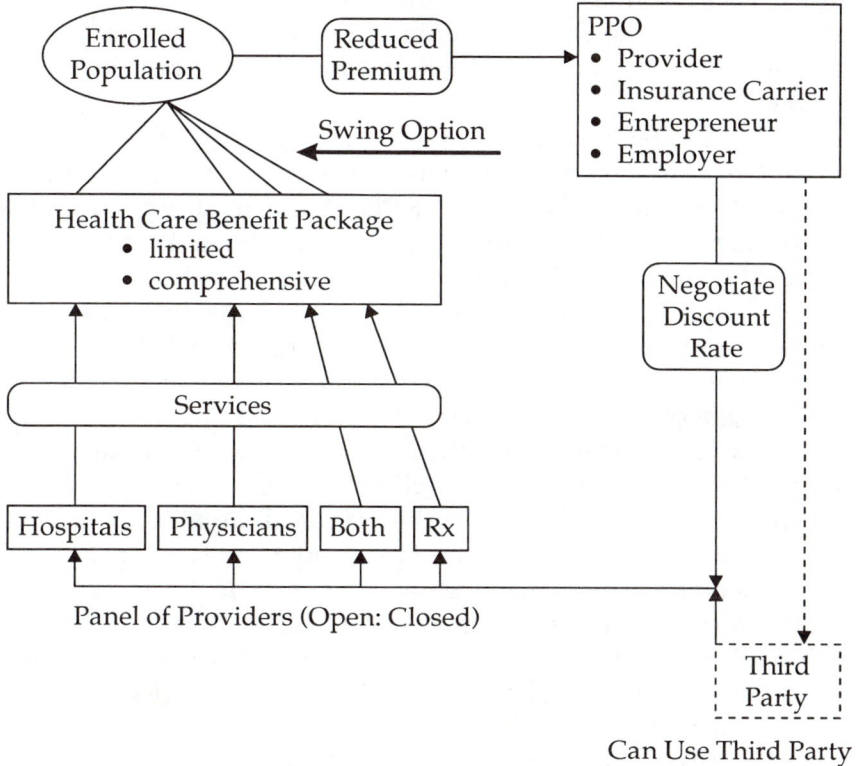

large managed care program exists. However, the provincial governments do not insist that all members of their population designate one particular provider as their provider. With separate, albeit controlled, budgets for physicians and hospitals, there have been few attempts to integrate the various resources into the "best" combination and size. The exceptions in Canada can be found in the development of HSOs and CHOs.

Health service organizations

As an outgrowth of the community health centers (CHCs), HSOs were developed in Ontario in the early 1980s (Lamb et al. 1991) as organizations sponsored by hospital, physician, or community groups that provide primary care to a voluntarily enrolled population. Reimbursement to the providers is made on a capitation basis. The voluntary nature of the enrollment extends to that of allowing clients to seek care either in or outside the system, and this applies not only to different episodes of care, but during any given episode.

This model might be seen as having disincentives for the providers to overserve the clients by incorporating a capitation payment (controls). However, without the requirement that all clients identify with one, and only one, provider, the control on the system breaks down. Clients *can* visit other providers at any time.

In an attempt to manage the system, the provider is put further at risk by what is termed "capitation negation" (Lamb et al. 1991). The third party payer, the provincial government, reduces the capitation payments if a registered client receives care outside the HSO. However, there is no penalty of any kind, such as a surcharge, placed on the client. Rather, it is expected that the primary care providers in the HSO will be able to persuade the clients to remain with the HSO and to not "shop around." A further attempt to manage the system is to be found in the ambulatory care incentive payment (ACIP)—(Lamb et al. 1991) the payment made to the HSO if it is determined that its clients used fewer inpatient services than the non-HSO population in the same geographic region.

The similarities between the HSO and the IPA-model HMO are readily apparent: the use of capitation, the capitation negation, and the bonus incentive tied to reduced hospital use. The only real difference is the very important one of controlling the total system by not placing restrictions on the client's use of primary care providers. The HSO, like the IPA-model only delivers primary care. An attempt to integrate the total system of care is found in the Canadian CHO model.

Comprehensive health organizations

In 1988, the Ontario Ministry of Health gave approval for the piloting of an experimental health care organization that would provide a comprehensive set of services in a vertically integrated

CHO. An example of the type of organization approved for development is the Toronto Hospital CHO. This CHO will provide and arrange for a comprehensive set of services that includes primary care, specialist care, hospital care, home care, social services, and where necessary, placement in a continuing care facility (Lamb et al. 1991). Primary care physicians in the family medicine centers in the hospital provide primary care and act as gatekeepers while the CHO contracts with all other necessary providers outside the existing hospital organization. The CHO receives a capitation payment for total care for each registered client from the provincial government.

Clients are not prevented from seeking care elsewhere, either for different episodes or within the same episode. The CHO is at risk for all of the costs incurred by its registered clients whether in or outside the plan.

The similarities of a CHO to the failed SAFECO experiment are quite remarkable. The provincial government has agreed to fund this project until the end of 1994.

The controls in this model are imposed entirely on the providers, and they are strong controls. Not requiring all registered clients to identify exclusively with the CHO increases scepticism from a total system control perspective. It is highly unlikely that a system that does not require that clients identify unequivocally with one provider organization can survive financially.

We have discussed case management and system management as separate and distinct entities, although in practice that is not necessarily the case because case management can play an important part in HMO-type of organizations.

Regionalization

The extent to which total system control has been attempted in both the United States and Canada, it has been applied to subsets of the population. Many organizations—such as major private health insurance companies like Blue Cross/Blue Shield and federal, state, and provincial governments, and major employers—have engaged in some form of managed care. In all cases, it has applied to some subset of the population such as enrollees, eligibles, or simply those who want to be included.

Regionalization is a system that organizes or manages all care or specific services for an entire population within geographically defined boundaries. The boundaries can be as all encompassing as regions of the country or as narrow as city boundaries. Region refers to the area in which the population to be served resides. The service delivery point need not be present in the defined region. In fact, the boundaries of the region may vary according to the type of service delivered. For example, a geographic region could be defined for the purpose of delivering perinatal services, but that geographic area could be combined with other geographic areas to define a region for delivering services to severely burned patients.

The economic concept of economies of scale discussed in Chapter 7 provides a rationale for regionalization. The extent to which economies of scale are present is the extent to which service-producing units should service a population that generates a demand large enough for the least cost size to be achieved. The work of Luft and his colleagues (Luft et al. 1990) has shown that for some procedures, in addition to the potential to reduce costs, greater volume is positively related to better outcomes.

In summary, we must recognize that different types of services generated by different resources may very well be substitutable in an episode of care. Chapter 7 presented examples of one particular human resource substituting for another human resource, and now we see how it is possible for one type of service to substitute for another service. It is also possible for a nonhuman resource to substitute for a human resource, at least to some extent. For example, the use of a new drug may substitute for some hospital care by reducing length of stay.

While no medical care system has achieved what has been suggested here and it is conceivable none ever will, the point is that a "best" combination and "best" size does exist, even if only in the abstract. When new organizational forms are tested in an attempt to reduce costs without reducing or perhaps increasing quality, they are searching for the Holy Grail—the "best" combination of resources and the "best" size of organization.

Discussion Questions

1. What are the differences between case management within a hospital and the gatekeeper model of case management, and

what are the relative strengths and/or weaknesses of the two models?

2. What are the mechanisms employed in an attempt to prevent organized systems of medical care delivery from overserving its members and from underserving members?

3. It is suggested in this chapter that, in order for an organized system of medical care delivery to be successful, clients must be required to identify with only one provider. Why is this essential, and what is the major cause for concern over this requirement?

4. Regionalization has the potential to achieve two highly desirable outcomes. What are they?

References

Fetter, R. B., Y. Shin, J. L. Freeman, R. F. Averill, and J. D. Thompson. "Case-Mix Definitions by Diagnosis Related Groups." *Medical Care* 18, supplement (1980): 1–53.

Hsaio, W. C., P. Braun, D. Yntema, and E. R. Becker. "Estimating Physicians' Work For a Resource-Based Relative Value Scale." *New England Journal of Medicine* 319 (September 1988): 835–41.

Hurley, R. B., and M. C. Fennell. "Managed-Care Systems as Government Structures: A Transaction Costs Interpretation." In *Innovations in Health Care Delivery: Insights for Organization Theory*, edited by S. M. Mick and Associates. San Francisco: Jossey-Bass, 1990.

Lamb, M., R. Deber, C. D. Naylor, and J. E. F. Hastings. *Managed Care in Canada: The Toronto Hospital's Proposed Comprehensive Health Organization.* Ottawa: Canadian Hospital Association Press, 1991.

Luft, H. S. "How Do Health Maintenance Organizations Achieve Their Savings?" *New England Journal of Medicine* 298 (15 July 1978): 1336–43.

Luft, H. S., D. W. Garnick, D. H. Mark, and S. J. McPhee. *Hospital Volume, Physician Volume, and Patient Outcomes.* Ann Arbor, MI: Health Administration Press, 1990.

Martin, D. P., J. L. Ehreth, and A. R. Geving. *A Case Study of United Healthcare.* Menlo Park, CA: The Henry Kaiser Family Foundation, 1985.

Merrill, J. "Defining Case Management." *Business and Health* (July-August 1985): 5–9.

Pauly, M. V. *Doctors and Their Workshops.* Chicago: University of Chicago Press, 1980.

Sloss, E. M., E. B. Keeler, and R. H. Brook, B. H. Operskalski, G. A. Goldberg, and J. P. Newhouse. "Effect of a Health Maintenance Organization on Physiologic Health: Results from a Randomized Trial." *Annals of Internal Medicine* 106 (1987): 130–38.

Ware, J. E., W. H. Rogers, A. R. Davies, G. A. Goldberg, R. H. Brook, E. B. Keeler, C. D. Sherbourne, P. Clamp, and J. P. Newhouse. "Comparison of Health Outcomes at a Health Maintenance Organization with Those of Fee-for-Service Care." *Lancet* (3 May 1986): 1017–22.

Figure 9.1 The Concept of Access

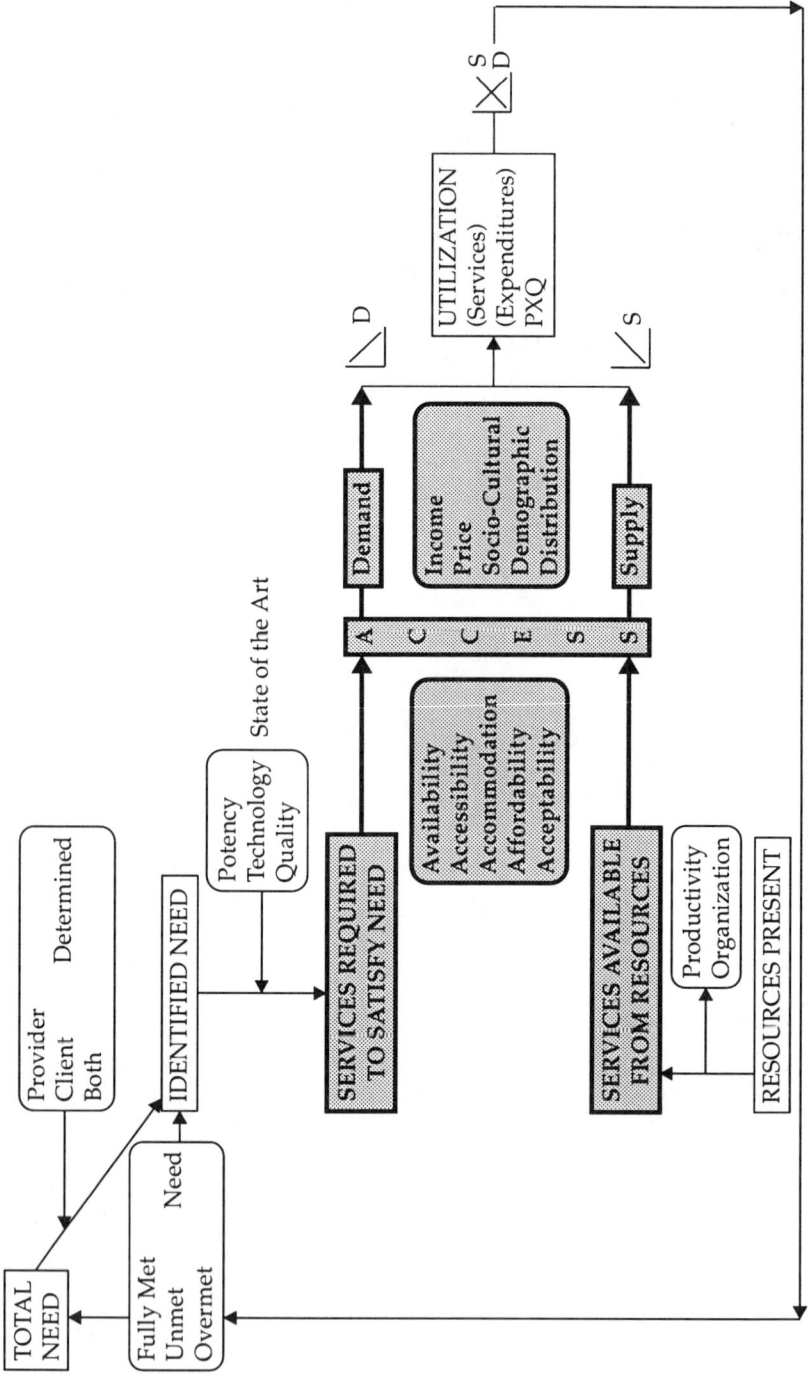

Chapter 9

Access

We have examined the processes by which to determine the number and type of services required in a given population, as well as those by which to determine the number and type of services available to that population. However, even if the number and type of services available are identical to the number and type of services required, the care may not be received by those who need it, and this is a major concern in the field of medical care delivery. Utilization occurs *only* when the characteristics of the provider (personnel and facilities) mesh with the characteristics of the client. Donabedian (1973) calls this the "fit" between the client and provider. Focusing on that part of the conceptual model shaded on the opposite page, access will be discussed in terms of this fit.

Integrating the Models of Access and Utilization

The degree to which there is a "fit" is the degree to which there is access. If we relax the condition that the number and type of services available are identical to the number and type required, access must also include the degree of fit between the number and type of services required and the number and type of services available. *Access* is, therefore, a multidimensional concept that includes a measure of availability but is not synonymous with availability. One of the most often encountered misconceptions in writings and research is to consider availability of services to constitute access.

To fully explore the several dimensions of access, we shall examine it through the lenses of several scholars' work. Donabedian's (1973) work brings to attention the many characteristics of the clients and the providers that either facilitate or are an impediment to access. It also emphasizes the fact that accessibility and availability are indeed separate concepts. Andersen (1968) in his seminal work in the development of a behavioral model of utilization, categorized the determinants into what he termed the "predisposing, enabling, and need" variables. Building on the work of Donabedian and Andersen, Penchansky and Thomas (1981) have provided a model that serves as an excellent blueprint for integrating the work of all of these scholars.

Donabedian (1973) introduces the notion of a set of factors intervening between the capacity to produce services and the actual production or consumption of services. These intervening factors are referred to as factors of accessibility or factors that influence the use of service. A subset of these factors is made up of the characteristics of the service or service-producing unit that render it more or less usable. This subset is further divided into socio-organizational variables and geographic variables, as presented in Figure 9.2.

Here, a service produced is equated with a service consumed. This is logical in a service industry because there can be no stockpiling or inventory-building. A service cannot be produced until it is consumed since a service describes an activity that takes place involving both the supplier and the consumer. For example, a barber is trained and equipped to cut hair, but he or she cannot

Figure 9.2   Interpretation of Donabedian's Model of Access

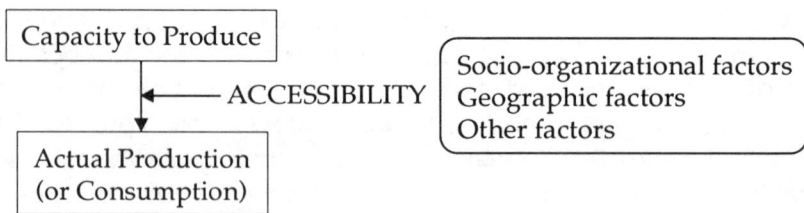

Source: Donabedian 1973.

provide the service until the client arrives on the scene to provide the hair to be cut. It may be more intuitive to consider the forces that may intervene between the services standing by in the form of service-producing units to produce an actual utilization of those services. Figure 9.2 identifies at least three types of intervening or accessibility, factors—socio-organizational, geographic, and other.

This interpretation lays the groundwork for a generalizable model of access integrating the important contributions of Andersen (1968) and Penchansky and Thomas (1981) to this field, as shown in Figure 9.3.

Andersen (1968) approached the concept of access from what might be described more as an economic perspective. He suggests that some consumers are predisposed toward using more medical care services than others and that this predisposition is acted on only to the extent that certain enabling conditions are fulfilled and the client perceives a need for care. These *predisposing* factors include sociodemographic variables such as age, sex, education, marital status, family size, race and ethnicity, and religious preference. The *enabling* variables include income, socioeconomic status, price of medical services, financing of medical services, and occupation. Andersen (1968) used several measures of *need* but found bed days disability to be the most appropriate one for his work.

Andersen (1968) described sets of factors viewed to determine utilization. Given that utilization only occurs to the extent that access has been achieved, utilization might be considered the interaction of demand and supply, with the determinants of

Figure 9.3   Generalizable Model of Access

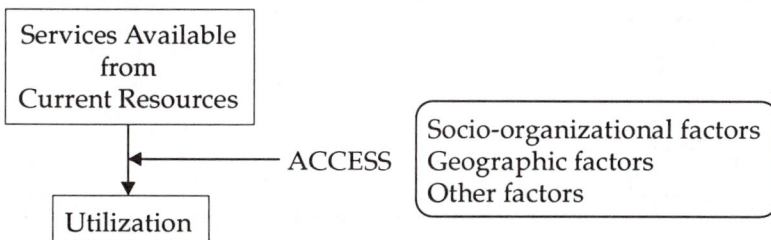

utilization subdivided into those of demand and those of supply. This is entirely consistent with Donabedian's (1973) notion of the meshing of these two sets of determinants, which he calls provider and client characteristics.

By recognizing that a characteristic may be present or absent in any given client or provider, we can then understand that these determinants might also be considered barriers to access. For example, if having enough money to pay for a medical care service determines utilization of that medical care service, then for an indigent client, money is a barrier to access. In addition, if providing evening office hours is a determinant of utilization, but the physician closes the office every afternoon at five o'clock, then office hours are a barrier to access. It is, of course, reasonable to conceive of these determinants as being partially present or partially absent, leading to partial access. Figure 9.4 interprets Andersen's model of utilization.

Both Donabedian (1973) and Andersen (1968) consider need to be a prerequisite to utilization, but where Andersen categorizes it as one of the determinants of utilization, Donabedian views it as the underlying sole determinant of services required. This difference is not the result of a different understandings of the role of need in the utilization of care, rather a function of the paradigms developed by the two scholars. Andersen (1968) argues that the client must first perceive a need, and Donabedian (1973) sees need translated into service equivalents required to address the need.

This text adheres closely to the Donabedian paradigm in that it treats need as the determinant of services required, which

Figure 9.4   Interpretation of Andersen's Model of Utilization

Source: Andersen 1968.

then become modified by access variables. The Donabedian and Andersen models are presented in Figure 9.5. To complete the integration, think of need as placed to the far left for Donabedian's model as an overarching, driving force, and included as one of the predisposing variables in Andersen's model.

Figure 9.5   Integration of the Andersen and Donabedian Paradigms

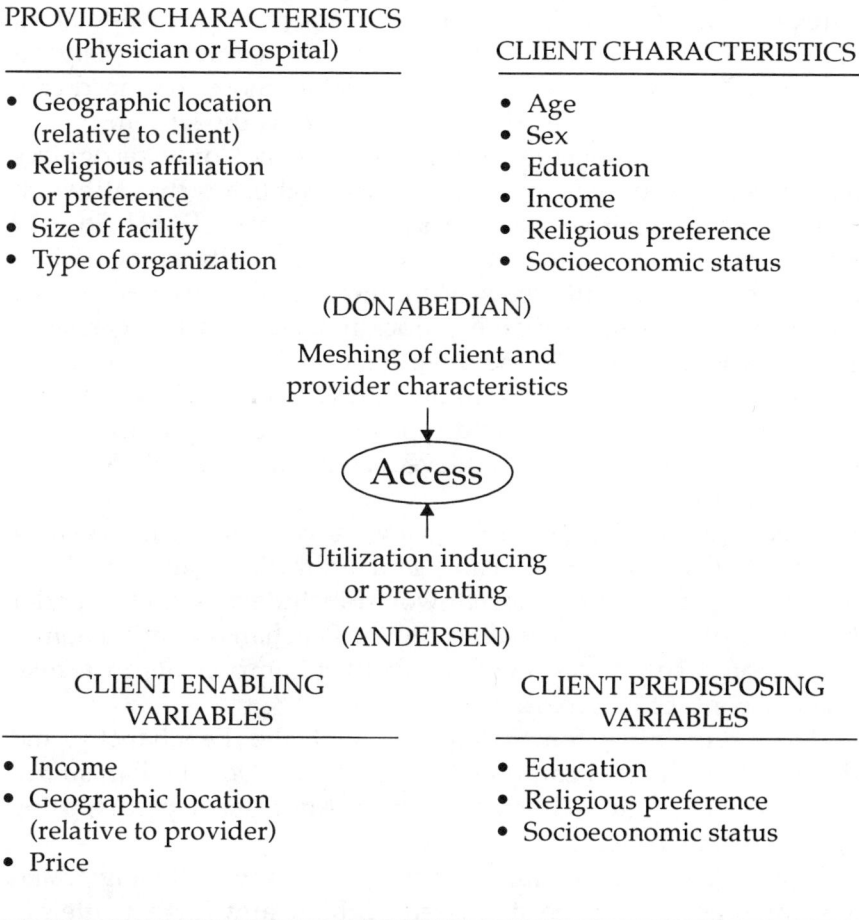

PROVIDER CHARACTERISTICS
  (Physician or Hospital)

CLIENT CHARACTERISTICS

- Geographic location
  (relative to client)
- Religious affiliation
  or preference
- Size of facility
- Type of organization

- Age
- Sex
- Education
- Income
- Religious preference
- Socioeconomic status

(DONABEDIAN)

Meshing of client and
provider characteristics

↓

(Access)

↑

Utilization inducing
or preventing

(ANDERSEN)

CLIENT ENABLING
VARIABLES

CLIENT PREDISPOSING
VARIABLES

- Income
- Geographic location
  (relative to provider)
- Price

- Education
- Religious preference
- Socioeconomic status

Sources: Andersen 1968; Donabedian 1973.

The Five A's of Access

Penchansky and Thomas (1981) also view access as a multidimensional concept and describe five dimensions, the names of which all begin with the letter A. This rather alliterative nomenclature provides us with the five A's of access—availability, accessibility, accommodation, affordability, and acceptability.

Availability

Availability is the fit between service capacity and the client's requirement. In our model, this concept is addressed by postulating that even if the volume and type of services required is identical to the volume and type of services available, those that need care may not get care—that is, they may not access the system.

This rather all-encompassing postulate not only recognizes that availability influences access, it also establishes that although the influence is positive, it is not necessarily proportional. So, a 10 percent increase in availability does not necessarily translate into a 10 percent increase in access. More importantly perhaps, an area with 10 percent less availability does not necessarily experience 10 percent less access. On the other hand, if full access is not necessarily achieved when the number and type of services available are identical to the number and type of services required, we can be certain that it cannot be achieved with less than this identical amount and type.

Because Donabedian (1973) views access as the intervening factor between services available and utilization, our model follows that logic. Andersen (1968) would include availability under the rubric of enabling variables, while Penchansky and Thomas (1981) would see it as one of the distinct components in a five-category concept of access.

The remaining four components of the Penchansky and Thomas (1981) model can now be linked with Donabedian's fit of provider and client characteristics and Andersen's predisposing and enabling variables.

Since the work of all of these scholars can be integrated as shown, access can be discussed without any further attempt to integrate their works. The four remaining categories in the Penchansky and Thomas model will be discussed.

Accessibility

Accessibility is the fit between the location of the provider and the location of clients according to Penchansky and Thomas (1981). Further consideration of the clients' transportation resources is given, resulting in the need to consider client travel distance, time, and cost.

In discussing the various aspects of geographic accessibility, we draw on more detailed reviews of the subject by Shannon, Bashshur, and Metzner (1969) and Donabedian (1973). However, before turning to the more tangible constructs of travel distance, time, and cost, the less tangible notion of perceived accessibility must be addressed. There is a distinct possibility that different populations may react to distance differently and, therefore, perceive accessibility differently. If, for example, a rural population regularly travels considerable distances in its normal daily living activities, it may not view traveling a long distance to receive medical care as an impediment to access. Or, a mile to a rural population's perception does not have the same inhibiting effect as a mile to an urban population.

Friction of space

A concept that will help us better grasp travel distance, time, and cost was introduced by ecologists following Robert Haig and reported in Hawley (1950). They introduced the term *friction of space*, which is the resistance felt by an object (or person) as it moves from point A to point B (see Figure 9.6). Figure 9.6 shows that while in all three cases the linear distance from point A to point B is the same, the travel distance is not. Compare this to Figure 9.7.

In Figure 9.7, client A lives much closer to facility C than does client B, but the travel distance is much greater for client A. Client A must travel on a rectangular route because there is no underpass at the critical point. Client B travels down Interstate 101, exits onto Interstate 92, and then exits immediately at the facility. Not only is the travel distance much greater for client A, but having to negotiate four stop lights makes the travel time even greater for client A.

Figure 9.6   Friction of Space

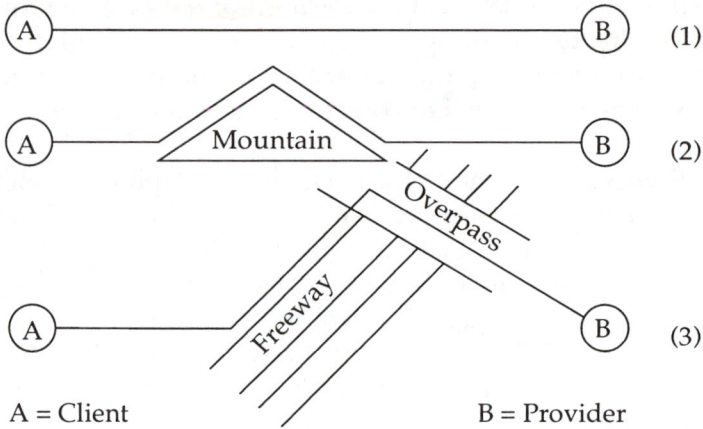

A = Client   B = Provider

While it might be readily apparent that one client may live closer to a facility yet have to travel further, it is perhaps not so intuitive that a client may live a shorter travel distance from the facility, yet incur a greater travel time. As Penchansky and Thomas (1981) point out, acknowledging the client's transportation resources may change the scenario completely. For example, it is not uncommon for state-of-the-art medical centers to be located in the heart of large metropolitan areas, areas that often encompass a large proportion of the indigent population. Quite often, an indigent population contains many elderly and incapacitated elderly. Not owning a car, these clients may have to rely on public transportation or the kindness of a family member or friend to travel to the facility. Therefore, even though the client may only live a quarter of a mile from the facility, it may take in excess of an hour to travel to the facility. Another client living miles away in the suburbs who owns a car needs far less time to get to the same facility.

Travel time and opportunity cost

The total cost of receiving care is a function of the service cost plus the opportunity cost. *Opportunity cost* can be thought of as

Figure 9.7 Travel Distance and Linear Distance

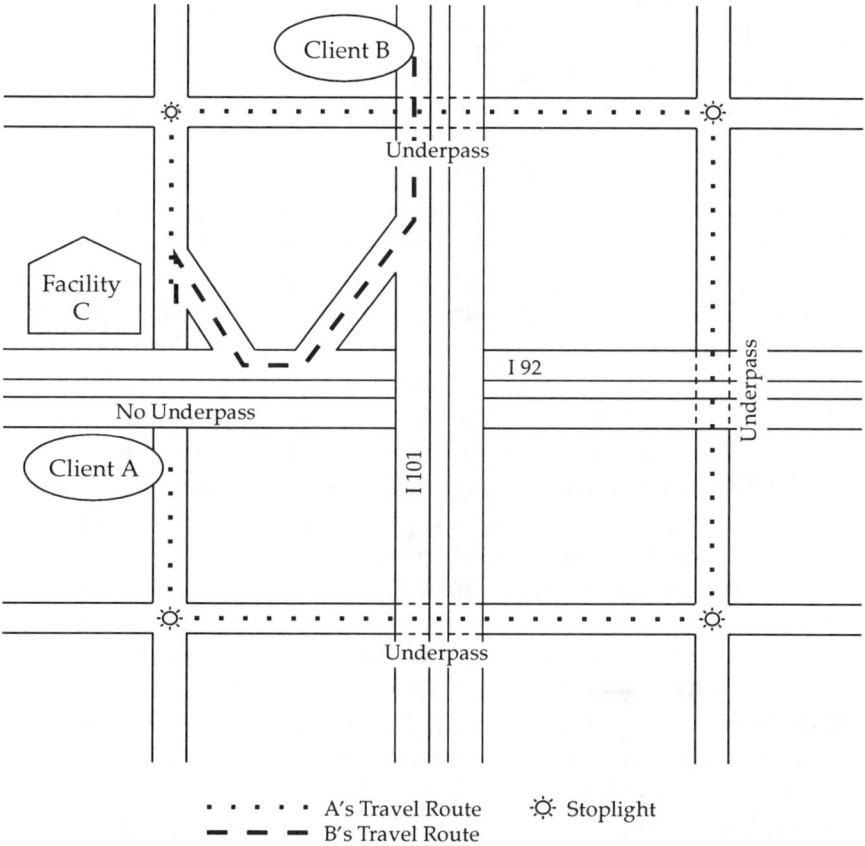

what is given up to receive care. In this case, the opportunity cost is represented by the travel time, and the amount of time involved in travel can be evaluated in terms of the other tasks that could have been accomplished in that time. This is not only a matter of accounting the amount of time involved but what each individual would be doing with that time if not traveling to receive care. It's misleading to think that the opportunity cost of someone not in the workforce might be less than that for someone in the workforce. The tasks that someone not employed in the workforce might be performing instead of traveling to receive care, such as home care or family care, have value that can be translated into opportunity cost. Plus, even if a member of the workforce is allowed time off with pay to travel to receive care, opportunity costs still exist.

Opportunity costs also apply to the waiting time that is part of the process of receiving care—after arrival at the care facility and before seeing a practitioner.

In planning hospital facilities for a given population, travel or opportunity costs are an important consideration in the overall access concerns. It is relatively simple to determine the number of beds appropriate for a population of a given size. The question, though, is whether those beds should be comprised in one or in multiple facilities. The more facilities used in employing a given number of beds, the shorter the average travel time, and therefore, the smaller the opportunity cost to the community (see Figure 9.8).

As illustrated, if it is determined that 450 beds are required to service the community, the average travel time if only one hospital is built (Community A) is much greater than if three hospitals of 150 beds each are built (Community B).

Economists who have investigated this phenomenon may agree that economies of scale are probably present in the hospital sector, and that therefore, the one large hospital is the better alternative. However, by considering opportunity costs to be those costs borne by society, it could be argued that in building one large hospital, the planners have engaged in cost-shifting—that is, some of the cost has been shifted from the provider to society. Depending on the shape of the two cost curves, the cost increase forced on society could be greater than the cost reduction realized by the provider. Figure 9.9 shows that at size S_1, the additional travel costs borne by society (AB) are greater than the cost reduction realized by the provider (BC). See Carr and Feldstein (1967) for a discussion of this phenomenon.

Affordability

The concept of affordability for most goods and services might simply be interpreted as the client's or consumer's ability to pay. But in the case of medical care services, the role played by health

Figure 9.8 Travel Time Relative to Facility Size

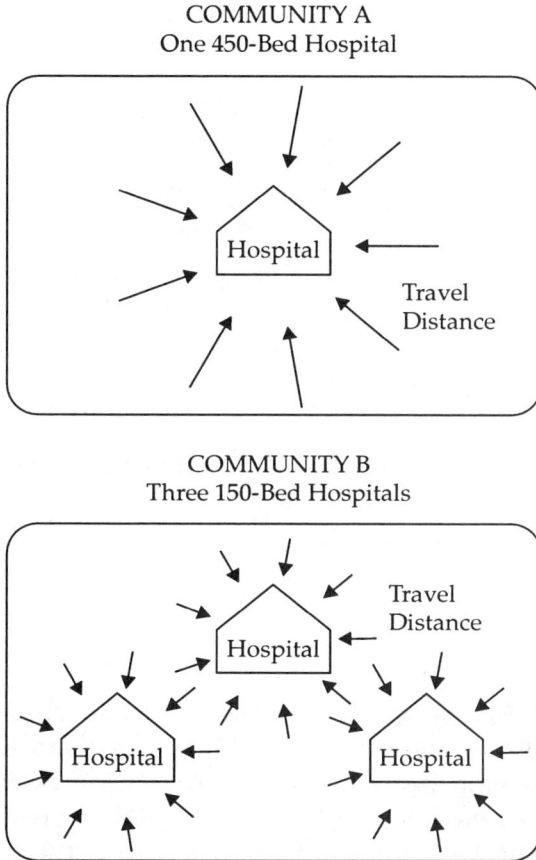

COMMUNITY A
One 450-Bed Hospital

COMMUNITY B
Three 150-Bed Hospitals

insurance has to be recognized. Its very presence masks the effect of income and price on the utilization of medical care services.

In deciding whether to utilize many other services, client perception of worth relative to total cost is of prime importance. In economic terms, clients consider marginal utility and the price relative to their incomes. Classical economics suggests that consumers will attempt to maximize their utility within their income constraints. This means that the less utility (worth) the clients perceive the service to have for them, the less they are willing

Figure 9.9   Economies of Scale and Opportunity Cost Trade-Off

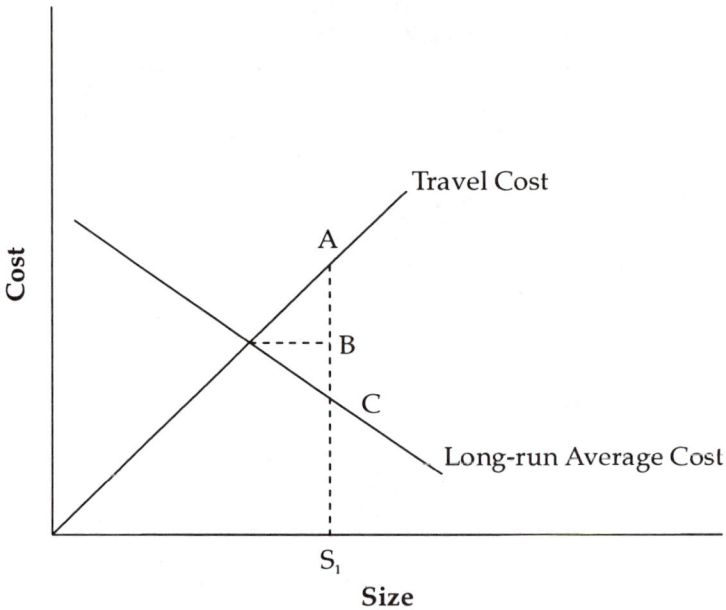

to pay for it. More importantly, the lower the price of the service, the less utility it has to have for clients for them to purchase it. We can, therefore, predict in the extreme case that if the service is priced at zero, clients will utilize the service even if it has no worth to them. This concept is extremely important in the context of this discussion because first-dollar coverage health insurance reduces the price of medical care services to zero at the point of consumption.

The traditional downward sloping demand curve is, in fact, a graphical representation of this relationship of marginal utility to price. First-dollar coverage places clients on the demand curve at the point at which it intersects the horizontal axis, zero price, as shown in point A in Figure 9.10. The pioneering experimental study by the Rand Corporation of the impact of coinsurance and deductibles demonstrated that the larger the out-of-pocket payment, the less medical care will be utilized (see Manning et al.

1987). In Figure 9.10, note how coinsurance raises the price above zero and consequently reduces utilization from $0 - q_a$ to $0 - q_b$.

A deductible typically requires that the client pay market price for the first units of consumption and then that price be reduced to zero beyond that utilization level. Referring to Figure 9.11, this means that those clients who are financially able to pay the equivalent of $p_c \times q_c$ will utilize the service to the same extent as would clients with first-dollar coverage—that is $0 - q_a$.

The fact that medical care services conform to the traditionally portrayed economic relationship between price and utilization has very important implications for access. As price is reduced, even to zero, utilization increases down the traditional, downward sloping demand curve. As discussed above, utilization will only increase to $0 - q_a$. Feldstein (1988) points out that if the need for care is such that a greater number of services are required, say $0 - q_n$, removing the price barrier altogether will not result in the

Figure 9.10   Demand for Medical Care and Health Insurance

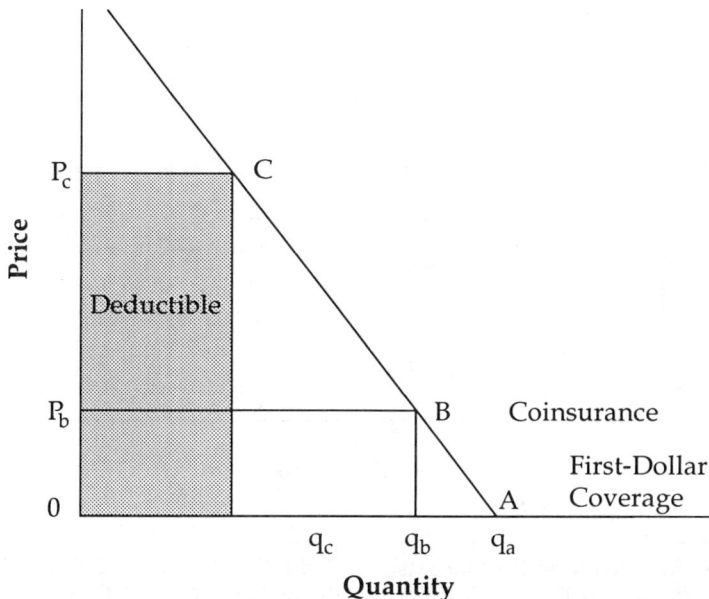

necessary utilization, as shown in Figure 9.11.

This classical economic model of demand for medical care services can provide the solution to this dilemma. By extending the demand curve below the horizontal axis to the point where it intersects the extended need curve, the amount that would have to be provided as a bonus to persuade those who need care to seek care can be determined. This is known as a negative price, and is shown in Figure 9.12.

However, this discussion has assumed that those clients demanding care would be the same clients needing care. Such an assumption requires an even greater leap of faith when clients are paid (receive a bonus) for receiving care. The approach of offering a bonus for receiving care is not altogether unheard of and

Figure 9.11   Demand and Need for Medical Care

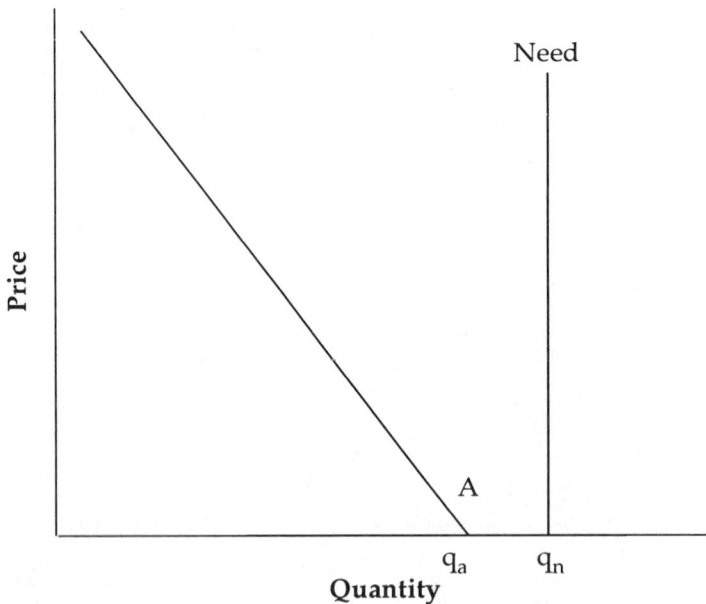

Note: Adapted form Paul J. Feldstein, *Health Care Economics*, 3d. ed. Reprinted with permission of Delmar Publishers, Albany, New York. © 1988.

Figure 9.12   The Meeting of Demand, Need, and Negative Price

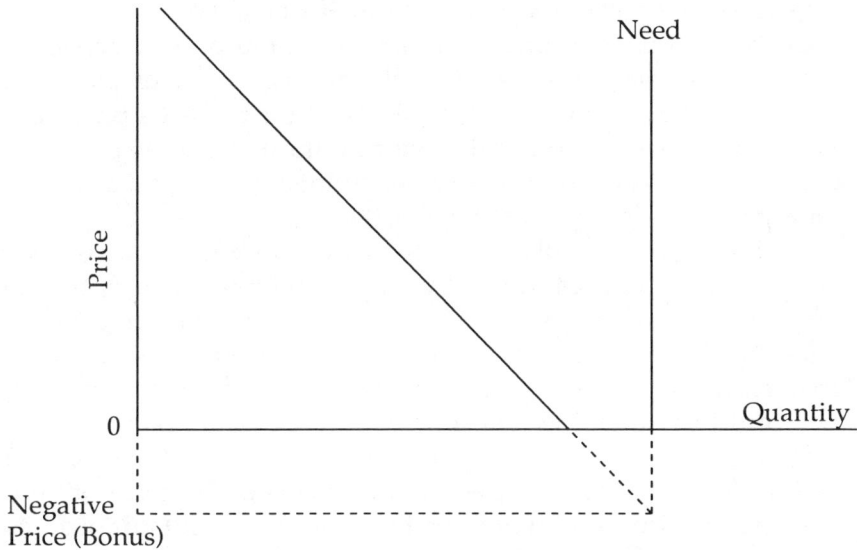

certainly not as outlandish as it may seem at first. For example, an HMO might adopt a similar practice in persuading members to undergo regular complete physical exams: to aid early detection, they might offer a bonus to all who comply with the established appropriate frequency of complete physical exams.

Accommodation

The fit between the manner in which resources are organized to supply services and the client's ability to take advantage of the arrangement is categorized by Penchansky and Thomas (1981) as *accommodation*. Included under this rubric are appointment systems, hours of operation, walk-in facilities, and telephone services. In its extreme form, accommodation is easy to understand, and the resulting utilization is predictable. If all physicians in a given area hold office hours only until five o'clock in the afternoon, all those in the population who must work until five o'clock will not be able to use physician services without considerable effort and lost human resource hours to society. If, on the other hand, the physicians have evening hours, even if only one or two days a week, their greater accommodation leads to improved access.

A variation on this concept is the provision of a telephone service. A client may not be able to take the time to visit a physician's office but may be able to take the time to make a telephone call and receive medical care advice. Telephone service is particularly appropriate in lieu of follow-up visits.

Although one could argue the extent to which this is a barrier to access, it is captured by the accessibility concept—more particularly, under opportunity cost. Accommodation, however, is meant to capture something in addition to what one must give up to receive care. Surely some clients, without regard for how else they could be spending that time, would be more likely to visit a physician if it were more convenient. Appointment systems and walk-in facilities could be placed at opposite ends of a continuum where either one could represent a barrier to or facilitator of access. For example, if the appointment system is scientifically developed and rigorously implemented, it could result in minimum wait-plus-service time in the physician's office. This could be an attractive feature to some clients and could therefore facilitate greater access to care. On the other hand, if the only way to see a physician is by appointment and the appointment system is neither scientifically developed nor rigorously implemented, it could be a barrier to access. Conversely, a walk-in system may be appealing, particularly for nonemergent conditions, if the client is willing and able to periodically "stop by."

The most accommodating of providers would likely have some evening hours, some daytime hours, some hours designated as walk-in hours, a scientifically developed and rigorously implemented appointment system for the nonwalk-in hours, and a telephone service.

Acceptability

Acceptability is based on the attitudes of both the client and the provider. Penchansky and Thomas (1981) suggest that *acceptability* is the fit between the clients' attitudes about the personal and practice characteristics of existing providers and providers' attitudes about the personal characteristics of the clients.

For example, clients may be concerned about the religious beliefs or affiliations of a provider. The provider in the case could be either human or facility or both. In turn, providers may be concerned about the religious beliefs of a client. For whatever reason, a Roman Catholic client may not find a Jewish hospital acceptable, or a Jewish client may not find a Roman Catholic hospital acceptable. In both of these examples, that particular hospital does not exist for the client. The client would ignore that hospital when needing treatment even if it were the closest appropriate facility to them.

In an interesting study, Morrill, Earickson, and Rees (1970) assessed the extra travel incurred by various ethnic and religious groups when seeking hospital care. Extra travel was defined as the travel beyond the facility closest to the client that was capable of treating the client's condition. The researchers cleverly captured the essence of this concept by quantifying the relative perception of linear distance traveled by the various groups. For example, because Jewish clients, apparently by choice, traveled three times as far to be treated in a Jewish hospital, it was suggested that they evaluated the distance to non-Jewish hospitals as being three times as far (Morrill, Earickson, and Rees 1970). Catholics evaluated the distance to non-Catholic hospitals as being twice as far as the distance to Catholic hospitals (Morrill, Earickson, and Rees 1970).

This study offers a quantifiable metric of acceptability and includes certain elements of accessibility previously discussed. Recall that in discussing friction of space, we considered the effort necessary to overcome the physical distance between a client and a provider. In examining acceptability, we are introduced to the concept of *perceived distance*. If we extrapolate, the notion of perceived effort to overcome perceived distance might be suggested. In other words, it might be that the Jewish clients in the Morrill, Earickson, and Rees (1970) study perceive the effort necessary to be treated in a Jewish hospital about the same as the effort necessary to be treated in a non-Jewish hospital that is only one-third of the distance from them. Obviously, the degree to which the facility is not acceptable is reflected in the magnitude of the extra distance clients are willing to travel.

An additional point of consideration is that clients do not always make the ultimate decision as to which hospital they will use. However, we can reasonably assume that physicians generally act in the best interests of their clients. If the physician has privileges in the hospital of the client's choice, we can assume that the physician will accommodate the client. Similarly, if a client feels strongly enough about his or her religious beliefs to prefer hospitals with the same religious affiliation, the client will, in all probability, seek out a physician with similar beliefs, who is more likely to have privileges in a hospital that is acceptable to the client.

Both clients and providers may have a variety of reasons or biases that, in their minds, make some providers, or clients, more acceptable than others. For example, in a study of live births in Baltimore hospitals, Studnicki (1975) sought to determine the characteristics of patients and hospitals that were associated with the deviation from the optimal accessibility model. Optimal accessibility, in this study, was described as the shortest travel time between the admitting hospital and the center of the census tract in which the client resided. Ethnic background was a major factor in explaining the average extra travel time.

Rubenstein, Mates, and Sidel (1977) recognize that age difference between the provider and client may also be a factor in explaining utilization and quality. They suggested that younger females may have received better care for urinary tract infection because of the similarity in age with the house staff.

Gender difference was cited by Mudd and Fleiss (1973) as a possible reason for less frequent performance of rectal and genital examinations on women. Because the physicians in the study were men the authors suggest that embarrassment on the part of the physician may have been a factor.

Again, it must be stressed that it is not a question of whether the provider refuses to treat certain clients, but one of whether the provider finds the client or the client finds the provider acceptable. The client may sense that the provider finds him or her unacceptable and feel uncomfortable, If the client feels uncomfortable for any reason, he or she probably will not return to that provider.

The discussion thus far has focused on the individual or the human provider. A facility may also be unacceptable to some clients. For example, Berki and Ashcraft (1980) suggest that social quality is an important factor in HMO enrollment. Social quality refers to "the physical attractiveness and social location of delivery sites" and "may include perceptions of the clientele the HMO serves [as well as] whom the patient shares the waiting room and clinical facilities with." In their excellent review of the literature, Berki and Ashcraft (1980) cite studies that have captured the dimensions of social quality variously by negative statements about the clinic atmosphere (Anderson and Sheatsley 1959; Tessler and Mechanic 1975).

The elements that determine and facilitate access can also be barriers to access. In considering this fact, it becomes patently clear that it is impossible to remove all barriers for all people. If the financial barrier to access is completely removed for everyone, there will be those who need care that will not receive care. While the accommodation barriers may be the easiest and least costly to remove, the most frequently addressed barrier is the financial one. It can be relatively easy to remove the financial barrier, but the cost for complete removal may be prohibitive. The removal of the friction of space barrier could be achieved by a more equitable distribution of resources and an improved or medical care system–dedicated transport system, neither of which is very likely.

The barrier that might prove to be the most difficult to remove completely is the acceptability barrier because it relies on individual, both provider and client, perceptions and beliefs that may be rational and consistently derived or irrational and idiosyncratic.

Discussion Questions

1. If the medical care system provided exactly the right number and type of medical care services that were required by the population, does this mean that those who require care will get care?

2. Accessibility refers to the relationship between the location of the provider and the location of the client. What important bearing does "friction of space" have on this component of access?

3. What trade-offs should be considered when planning the size of a service delivery unit relative to the population it serves?

4. First-dollar coverage renders medical care services free at the point of consumption. According to marginal benefit analysis, what problems might result from this?

5. What are Penchansky and Thomas' five A's of access?

References

Andersen, R. *A Behavioral Model of Families' Use of Health Services.* Research Series 25. Chicago: University of Chicago Press, 1968.

Anderson, O. E., and P. B. Sheatsley. *Comprehensive Medical Insurance: A Study of Costs, Use and Attitudes under Two Plans.* Research Series G. Chicago: Health Information Foundation, 1959.

Berki, S. E., and M. L. F. Ashcraft. "HMO Enrollment: Who Joins What and Why? A Review of the Literature." *Milbank Memorial Fund Quarterly/Health and Society* 58 (1980): 588–632.

Carr, W. J., and P. J. Feldstein. "The Relationship of Cost to Hospital Size." *Inquiry* 4 (1967): 45–65.

Donabedian, A. *Aspects of Medical Care Administration: Specifying Requirements for Health Care.* Cambridge, MA: Harvard University Press for the Commonwealth Fund, 1973.

Feldstein, P.J. *Health Care Economics,* 3d ed. New York: John Wiley & Sons, 1988.

Hawley, A. H. *Human Ecology: A Theory of Community Structure.* New York: Ronald Press, 1950.

Manning, W. G., J. P. Newhouse, N. Duan, E. B. Keeler, A. Leibowitz, and M. S. Marquis. "Health Insurance and the Demand for Medical Care: Evidence from a Randomized Experiment." *American Economic Review* 77 (June 1987): 251–77.

Morrill, R., R. J. Earickson, and P. Rees. "Factors Influencing Distance Traveled to Hospitals." *Economic Geography* 46 (April 1970): 161–71.

Mudd, J. W., and J. L. Fleiss. "Physical Examinations of Hospitalized Adults." *Journal of Medical Education* 48 (1973): 1140–47.

Penchansky, R., and J. W. Thomas. "The Concept of Access: Definitions and Relationship to Consumer Satisfaction." *Medical Care* 19 (February 1981): 127–40.

Rubenstein, L., S. Mates, and V. W. Sidel. "Quality-of-Care Assessment by Process and Outcome Scoring—Use of Weighted Algorithmic Assessment Criteria for Evaluation of Emergency Room Care of Women with Symptoms of Urinary Tract Infection." *Annals of Internal Medicine* 86 (1977): 617–25.

Shannon, G. W., R. L. Bashshur, and C. A. Metzner. "The Concept of Distance as a Factor in Accessibility and Utilization of Health Care." *Medical Care Review* 26 (February 1969): 143–61.

Studnicki, J. "The Minimalization of Travel Effort as a Delineating Influence for Urban Hospital Service Areas." *International Journal of Health Services* 5 (1975): 679–93.

Tessler, R., and D. Mechanic. "Factors Affecting Choice between Prepaid Group Practice and Alternative Insurance Programs." *Milbank Memorial Fund Quarterly/Health and Society* 54 (1975): 149–72.

Figure 10.1 System and Client Outcomes

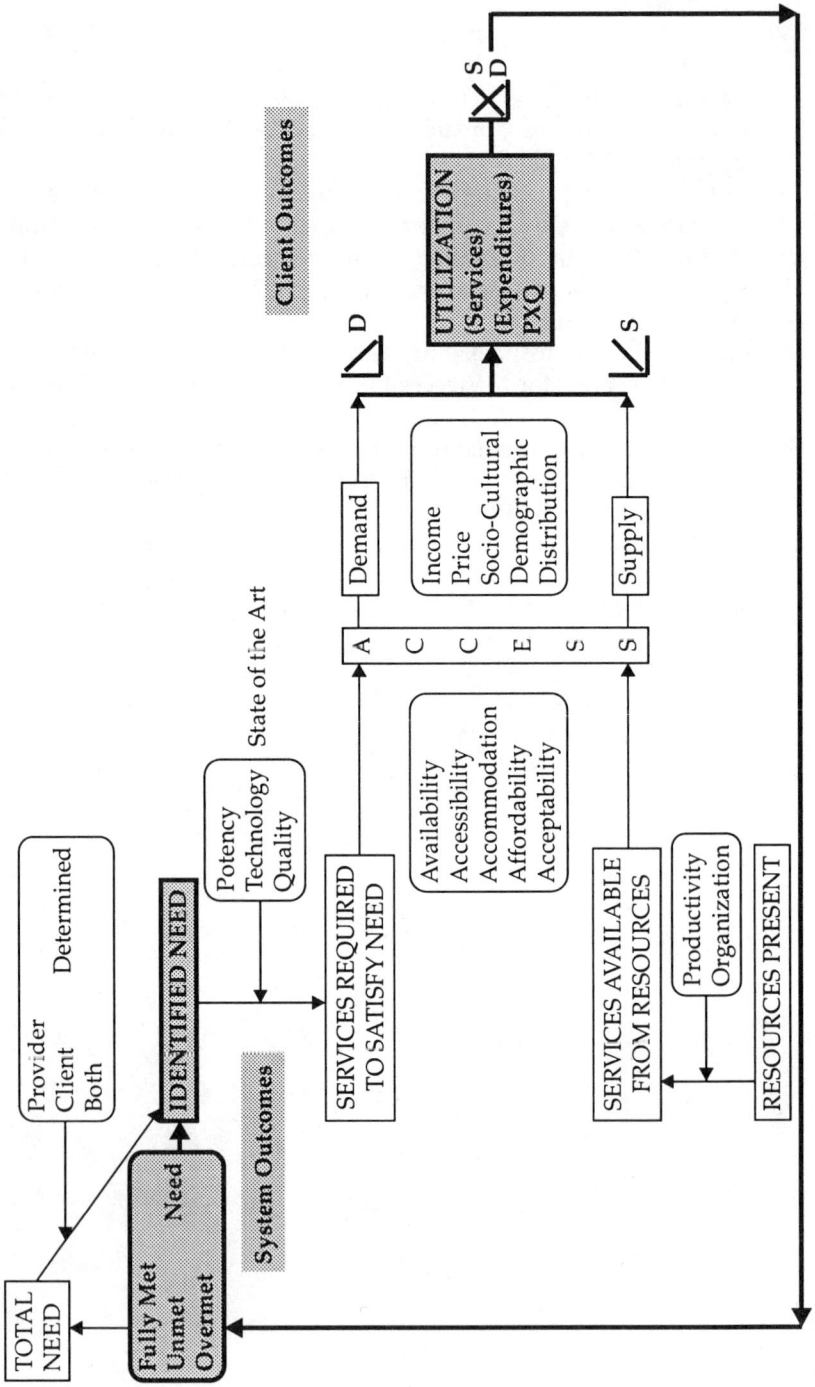

Chapter 10

Outcome Measures

We have discussed the manner in which need can be translated into services required and the manner in which resources can be translated into services available. We have further considered the concept of access that can be viewed in terms of the extent to which utilization is impeded or enhanced. We now consider perhaps the most important element of any medical care system or subsystem—the outcomes of the system.

If we consider two types of outcomes this text will be more readily understood and some of the confusion that permeates most discussion of medical care outcomes may be clarified. The two types are *system outcomes* (see shaded in the model on the opposite page) and *client outcomes* (see shaded in the model).

This chapter argues that expenditures can be defined as price of services multiplied by the quantity of those services utilized. As such, expenditures can be considered a measure of output or an outcome of the system. Components of national health care expenditures in the United States and Canada are compared and followed by other comparisons of the quantity of services in both countries. The chapter then discusses client outcomes in terms of population-based measures such as mortality rates and life expectancy and then considers patient-specific clinical outcomes. Consistent with the conceptual model, quality-of-life measures are discussed as an outcome measure that might be considered an attenuation of client-defined need. This leads into an examination of the extent to which need has been ameliorated, or fully met, overmet, or undermet. Finally the ways the components of the conceptual model can be used to define a medical care utilization function are described.

System Outcomes

System outcomes are those outcomes that measure something other than the health status of individuals or populations. They might be thought of as intermediate outcomes, although they may manifest themselves concurrently with the health status type of outcomes. In other words, utilization of services and health status changes may occur simultaneously, but it is not intuitively unreasonable to accept that utilization occurs first and health status changes follow. One of the most often used measures of system outcomes is that of health care expenditures.

Health care expenditures

Health care expenditures are completely analogous to the sales volume concern in other sectors of the economy and therefore are part of our daily activities and mind-set. Whether nationwide or for a subsector or whether for one service or all services, *health care expenditures* are nothing more than the price of services multiplied by the quantity utilized (P × Q). As simple as it may seem, it is significant to acknowledge that it is probably easier to reduce quantity than it is to reduce price when attempting to reduce health care expenditures.

   In my opinion, there are still those who look on health care expenditures, particularly per capita expenditures, as some measure of output of the health care system. This is consistent with a sales volume approach to evaluating any industry that does not make the connection between the amount purchased and the benefit derived by the consumer. With this kind of mind-set it is easier to generate a receptive environment for health care expenditure reduction because it is not associated with the potential to reduce health status. There may indeed be legitimate reasons for wanting to reduce health care expenditures, but to simply concentrate on the magnitude of the expenditures ignores the real reason for using the service—that is, to improve health status or well-being. To say that we must reduce health care expenditures is no more noble than to say that we must spend more. Whether analyzed in dollar amounts or in percent of gross domestic product (GDP) makes little difference. For example, if it could be demonstrated that by spending 20 percent of GDP on medical care, the population was three times as healthy as when only 10 percent of GDP was spent, would that not represent a desirable state of affairs?

As suggested in Chapter 1, the overriding concern should be for accountability or contribution to an improved state of health, however measured. We assume that for other goods and services, the consumer, who is also the purchaser, perceives some value added when consuming or utilizing the good or service. Would we be concerned if 15 percent of GDP was spent on color television sets?

It is, of course, appropriate to address the issue of increasing expenditures on medical care for two compelling reasons: (1) we have a right, as individuals, to expect perceived value for our money as previously mentioned; (2) more often than not, it is other people's money—or more accurately, it is part of a risk-pooling arrangement or mandatory government system that requires everyone to help pay for the medical care of others. These third parties are now beginning to demand accountability.

With this in mind, and without intending to indulge in a detailed explication of national health care expenditures, some of the more salient components are presented in Table 10.1.

Table 10.1 National Health Care Expenditures in the United States and Canada

	United States (1990)	Canada (1990)
Total health care expenditures	$ 675b	$ 62b
Personal health care expenditures	592b	55b
Personal health care expenditures/capita	2,279	2,068
Expenditures for hospital care	258b (38%)	25b (39%)
Expenditures for physician care	129b (19%)	9b (15%)
Drugs and other nondurables	56b (8%)	8b (13%)
Percent of GDP	12.2%	9.4%

b = billions.
Sources: Health and Welfare Canada 1992; Letsch et al. 1990.

While always a temptation to compare cross-nationally, the problems inherent in simply comparing percent of GDP devoted to medical care are many. Although population numbers and characteristics change over time, a more valid comparison for the purposes of this discussion is one that compares the same country over time, as Table 10.2 does.

Although the data in Table 10.2 are not adjusted for inflation, meaningful comparisons of changes over time can be made. The growth of total health care expenditures in the period 1975–1990 in the United States was 408 percent, and in Canada, 417 percent. The growth in per capita expenditures was 339 percent in the United States and 336 percent in Canada. The overall inflation rate must have been greater in Canada during this period because expenditures as a percentage of GDP increased only 31 percent in Canada compared to 47 percent in the United States. If inflation averaged 5 percent a year, we would expect to see a growth rate of 200 percent. That is, expenditures in 1990 would be double the 1975 figure. In both countries this was exceeded by quite a large amount.

The important point for our purposes is whether, given a large increase in this output measure, the health status of the population in both countries improved during that period.

Table 10.2 Growth in National Health Care Expenditures in the United States and Canada, 1975–1990

	United States		Canada	
	1975	1990	1975	1990
Total health care expenditures	$133b	$ 675b	$ 12b	$ 62b
Per capita expenditures	592	2,601	540	2,357
Percent of GDP	8.3	12.2	7.3	9.4
Expenditures for hospital services	52b	258b	5b	25b
Expenditures for physician services	23b	129b	2b	9b
Expenditures for drugs and other medical nondurables	13b	56b	1b	8b

b = billions.
Sources: Lazenby and Letsch 1990; Letsch et al. 1990; Health and Welfare Canada 1992.

The changing nature of the two systems is apparent by study-ing Table 10.2. When the components are viewed as a percentage of total expenditures, the dynamics of the two countries differed somewhat. In the United States, the hospital share remained fairly constant at 38 percent. The physician share increased by two per-centage points (17 to 19 percent), and drug expenditures decreased by two percentage points (10 to 8 percent). In Canada, the hospital share dropped from 44 to 39 percent, the physician share remained approximately the same (15 percent), and drug expenditures in-creased four percentage points (9 to 13 percent).

When comparing the source of expenditures in the two sys-tems, over time, it can be seen that the public-private split in the United States has remained relatively constant over the 15-year period 1975–1990 (42:58), while the split in Canada shows some movement toward relatively greater private expenditures (76:24 to 72:28).

Quantity of services

Because expenditures are simply the price of a service multiplied by the quantity of services used, Table 10.3 supplies data on mea-sures of service use in the United States and Canada.

Client Outcomes

Whereas system outcomes refer to the medical care services pro-duced or expenditures on medical care (intermediate outcomes), client outcomes refer to the impact that medical care has on a client's health status. It is perhaps necessary to modify client

Table 10.3 Selected Medical Care Service Use: United States and Canada, 1990

	United States	Canada
Admissions (percent of population)	13.7	14.1
Average length of stay	9.1 days	13.9 days
Hospital service use bed days/capita	1.2 days	2.0 days
Physician services contacts/person	5.5	6.9

Source: Schieber, Poullier, and Greenwald 1993.

outcomes even further to consider population measures and individual measures of health status. In other words, given that the medical care system exists only to improve or sustain the health status of individuals and therefore the population it serves, client outcomes are designed to capture this contribution. Table 10.4 provides data on selected population outcome measures in the United States and Canada.

In terms of infant mortality, the United States ranked 20th of the 24 country members of the Organization for Economic Cooperation and Development (OECD). The only countries ranked below the United States were New Zealand, Greece, Portugal, and Turkey. Canada ranked seventh on this measure behind Japan, Sweden, Finland, Iceland, Netherlands, and Switzerland (Schieber, Poullier, and Greenwald 1993).

Life expectancy at birth for males in the United States ranked 17th, Canada ranked 10th. For females, the United States ranked 16th, and Canada ranked 7th. Life expectancy at age 80 is suggested as a better measure of the efficacy of the medical care system: the United States ranked second for males and third for females; Canada ranked second for both sexes. For this measure, the only countries to perform better than the United States were Switzerland and Iceland; Iceland was the only country to outperform Canada.

Table 10.4   Selected Health Outcome Measures in the United States and Canada

	United States (1990)	Canada (1990)
Infant mortality rates (deaths/1,000 live births)	9.1	6.8
Life expectancy at birth		
Male	72.0 years	73.8 years
Female	78.8 years	80.4 years
Life expectancy at 80 years		
Male	7.1 years*	7.1 years
Female	9.0 years*	9.3 years

* = 1989.
Source: Schieber, Poullier, and Greenwald 1993.

Using these types of measures as outcome measures reveals the marginal relationship between medical care spending and population outcomes. In fact, Schieber, Poullier, and Greenwald (1993) calculated the simple, zero order correlation of per capita expenditures and these outcome measures in the 24 OECD countries, as shown in Table 10.5. The problem with this type of analysis is that the outcome measures are influenced by many things other than the use of medical care services. (In Chapter 1 we discussed this in considerable detail.) To put it another way, these very gross outcome measures are not very sensitive to medical care utilization, resulting in the conclusion that either we are measuring the wrong thing or our medical care system is not very efficacious.

Is there any solution to this dilemma? We could look at individual disease or illness conditions and determine whether the prevalence and incidence of those conditions were being affected. Unfortunately, we still could not be certain with many disease conditions that an increase in prevalence and incidence was the result of poor medical care or that a decrease was the result of good medical care. This point is clarified by the dramatically increasing incidence and prevalence of AIDS.

With some disease conditions, particularly at the individual level, it can be demonstrated unequivocally that the intervention

Table 10.5   Correlation of Expenditures per Capita and Selected Outcome Measures in 24 OECD Countries, 1988

	Correlation Coefficient
Per capita spending and infant mortality rates	−0.49
Per capita spending and perinatal mortality rates	−0.53
Per capita spending and life expectancy at birth	
Males	0.42
Females	0.52
Per capita spending and life expectancy at 80 years	
Males	0.57 n.s.
Females	0.73

n.s. = not statistically significant.
Source: Schieber, Poullier, and Greenwald 1993.

of medical care services restores health status to its expected level. For certain conditions, expected level of health status would include slowing or halting the progression of the disease. We know that medical care intervention can have a dramatic, positive effect in individual cases; consider joint replacement, organ transplants, and major traumatic events, for example. However, in the overall scheme of things, these events represent a very small component of medical care system.

Therefore, within the model presented herein need must be unequivocally defined and the services required to address need must be identified. Only then will specific need-sensitive services be delivered and the full impact of those services legitimately measured in terms of the attenuation of the identified need. This is true whether the focus is on a specific need—that is, one illness condition—or all needs in the population. Remember that we have referred to need in terms of conditions requiring all types of services, including public health and preventive services. Defining need is the very foundation of the medical care system. Whether it is a measure of a particular illness or total illness in the population, a particular lack of well-being or total lack of well-being, or the need for a particular preventive service or the total need for preventive services, agreement on what constitutes need is absolutely essential. Without agreement, the chances of ameliorating need are very small.

Quality-of-Life Outcomes

In Chapter 4 we discussed the concepts of provider- and client-defined need. The profound difference in the way these actors define the need for medical care is to some degree responsible for the lack of universally accepted outcome measures. A medical care intervention that eradicated a pathological deficiency but left the patient not feeling well would be viewed very differently by the client and the provider.

There can be no question that we are becoming more enlightened in this regard and that more attention is being paid to the nonclinical outcomes of medical care. Such measures as *quality of life* are being assessed, often in conjunction with clinical outcomes, after a medical care intervention. A plethora of instruments and methodologies have been engaged to determine whether a client's life is better as the result of the medical care. While it is not the purpose of this book to examine these methodologies in detail, a cursory look at two of the more frequently used measures is in order.

The *time trade-off* technique measures the number of years of life a client would be willing to give up in exchange for life of complete well-being. The more years the client would be willing to sacrifice, the lower his or her quality of life. For example, if the life expectancy of the client is 40 years, but he or she is experiencing a poor quality of life due to health problems, the interviewer attempts to find the indifference point, or the number of years spent in complete well-being as opposed to 40 years in the current condition. So, someone who is willing to give up 20 years of life has a much lower quality of life than someone who is only willing to give up 5 years. See Torrance (1976) for a discussion on the time trade-off technique.

The *standard gamble* is a somewhat similar technique. The indifference point in this methodology is the probability of death that the client would willingly accept in exchange for a life of complete well-being. The client is asked whether he or she would willingly undergo a procedure that had a specified probability of death (e.g., $p = 0.20$) and a specified $(1 - p)$ probability of being made completely well. In this case, someone who is willing to accept a 40 percent chance of death has a much lower quality of life than someone who is only willing to accept 5 percent chance of death. See Torrance (1987) for an application of the standard gamble technique in health care.

There are many variations of these techniques, and by design, only very perfunctory descriptions have been provided. All quality-of-life measures, however, could be approaches to measuring the nonclinical determinants of wellness. If they are used in conjunction with clinical outcomes assessment measures, we may begin to address both the provider-defined and the client-defined needs for care.

Unmet, Fully Met, and Overmet Need

The extent to which identified need has been addressed is also a significant factor. Need can be *fully met*—need has been appropriately addressed by the services provided—or can be *overmet*—more services were provided than were necessary to address the need—or *unmet*—need was not addressed either by enough services or service at all. Fully met need does not imply that the need for care has been eliminated, rather that the appropriate number and type of services were provided. These categories of need are consistent with the "flat of the curve" phenomenon presented in Chapter 1 (see Figure 1.5). Unmet need is represented by any part of the curve above the current position but below the inflection point (where the curve flattens out); fully met need is represented by the inflection point; and overmet need is any point on the flat of the curve.

While much of the research and administrative activity is now devoted to identifying and eliminating overmet need, there is growing concern to identify and address unmet need. A major step in this direction can be achieved by the removal of any of the barriers discussed in Chapter 9. Although the financial barrier is only one of several barriers to access, the increasing numbers of uninsured and underinsured in the United States is a major contributor to the unmet need in that population.

The Utilization Function

For the final perspective on outcomes in this discussion, we draw on the classical demand function, the Andersen (1968) model of medical care utilization, and the elements of our model.

The classic demand function can be written as:

$$q_x = f(p_x, p_y, p_z, I, T, W)$$

where: q_x = quantity of service x, p_x = price of service x, p_y = price of service y (substitutes), p_z = price of service z (complements), I = Income, T = Taste, and W = Wealth.

Andersen's (1968) model can be written as:

$$U_{mc} = f \text{ (enabling variables, predisposing variables,}$$
$$\text{need)}$$

where: U_{mc} = utilization of medical care; enabling variables = price, income, wealth, geographic location, etc.; predisposing variables

= sociodemographic variables, etc.; and need = need for medical care.

It is not much of a stretch to integrate these two models together, requiring only that we broaden our definition of *taste* to include something that is desired, whether it feels good or not. For example, a person with a broken arm may be someone who has a greater "taste" for medical care than a completely healthy person. To the extent that sociodemographic variables are considered proxies for need, they too can be viewed as part of the taste argument in the demand function. For example, an 80-year-old person may have a greater "taste" for medical care than a 20-year-old.

In synthesizing the two models, enabling variables would include the price, income, wealth, and locational variables. Taste can be represented by the need and the sociodemographic variables and can be included under the rubric of predisposing variables. The function for medical care utilization can now be written:

$$U_{mc} = f \text{ (economic variables [E], locational variables}$$
$$\text{[E], sociodemographic variables [P][T],}$$
$$\text{need [P][T])}$$

where: E = enabling variables, P = predisposing variables, T = taste variables.

Our model graphically presents this utilization function, and is a blueprint for specifying a utilization or demand model.

We have now come full circle in our model by considering how well the identified need for medical care was met. All that remains for us is to challenge the validity of the model as a representative of a medical care system. This will be accomplished in the next chapter by considering the model's utility in placing government intervention in context and its applicability to all types of medical care.

Discussion Questions

1. What is the relationship between system outcome measures and client outcome measures?

2. Client outcome measures might be viewed as provider-determined or client-determined. What are examples of these two types of outcome measure and what are the implications of their uses?

3. How can this conceptual model help define a medical utilization function?

References

Andersen, R. *A Behavioral Model of Families' Use of Health Services*. Research Series 25. Chicago: University of Chicago Press, 1968.

Health and Welfare Canada. Health Information Division of the Policy, Planning and Information Branch. *Health Expenditures in Canada*. Ottawa, Ontario: Health and Welfare Canada, 1993.

Lazenby, H. C., and S. W. Letsch. "National Health Expenditures, 1989." *Health Care Financing Review* 12 (Winter 1990): 1–35.

Letsch, S. W., H. C. Lazenby, K. R. Levit, and C. A. Cowan. "National Health Expenditures." *Health Care Financing Review* 14 (Winter 1992): 1–30.

Schieber, G. J., J. P. Poullier, and L. M. Greenwald. "Health Spending, Delivery and Outcomes in OECD Countries." *Health Affairs* 12 (Summer 1993): 120–29.

Torrance, G. W. "Social Preferences for Health Status: An Empirical Evaluation of Three Measurement Techniques." *Socio-Economic Planning Sciences* 10 (1976): 128–36.

———. "Utility Approach to Measuring Health Related Quality of Life." *Journal of Chronic Disease* 40 (1987): 593–600.

Chapter **11**

Generalizability and Utility
of the System Model

Theory is one of the most powerful tools for generalizing. Any social system with the complexity of the medical care system is rightfully subject to critical examination and evaluation from a myriad of disciplines. Given this multidisciplinary nature and the fact that no one unifying theory of medical care exists, a conceptual model is perhaps the next best thing. This is true, of course, only if the model has generalizability and utility—that is, can it apply to all possible medical care services as well as the total system, and does it serve any useful purpose?

In this chapter we take examples from each of what might be considered the three major generic components of the medical care system—preventive care, acute care, and long-term care—and discuss their "fit" with the conceptual model (generalizability). We then take examples of public policy in the health care field and discuss their placement in the conceptual model and trace their impact throughout the system (utility). It is not possible in ten, or even 100 volumes, to consider how all possible medical care services might fit the model, but briefly examining different service types will help us understand how well the model works.

To address the generalizability of the model, three quite distinct types of medical care service are discussed: public health or preventive services, acute care services, and long-term care services.

161

Preventive Medical Care Services

Primary prevention such as vaccination programs and early detection programs such as any of the established screening programs are considered to be representative of this service type. Since establishing or identifying need is critical to the functioning of the medical care system and to the integrity of the model, the definition of need is variable, depending on who defines it. If this premise is accepted, it becomes very simple to define the need for these types of service.

If part, or all, of the population is at risk for polio or influenza, then there is a need for a vaccination program. This can be translated into the number and type of resources required to generate the vaccination service by considering the combination of resources and the size of the program necessary to deliver such a service. Providing a program, however, does not guarantee that those at risk will use the service. All of the potential barriers to access exist for this service; in fact, it has been shown that with preventive services, barriers become more of a burden. The extent to which the service is utilized by the population at risk will indicate the amount of utilization and, therefore, unmet need. Freeman et al. (1987) report on the potential underuse of preventive-type service by income status.

State of the art medical care would dictate that certain sectors of the population should receive a pap smear, a mammography, or regular physicals that include a thorough examination of the prostate. All of these services represent need in the respective subpopulations. Although there may be no pathological deficiency in the individuals screened in this way, the actual screening service represents provider-defined need.

Acute Care Services

Because acute care is the care that immediately comes to mind when most individuals are forced to confront the medical care system, it might have seemed that this text focused on acute care, which would make it much easier to fit acute care into our model. However, additional points must be made.

As discussed earlier, for some disease conditions (diabetes, for example) there may be no cure, but certain medical services are capable of sustaining the individual in that disease state for a normal lifetime. For some disease conditions (like AIDS), not only is there no cure, but medical care services are only capable of sustaining life for a relatively short period. In these cases while medical care service cannot eradicate the need, the services are still required. These needs can be translated into the requirement for a certain number and type of resource. All of the problems of access pertain to and, in some cases, are even accentuated by fear on the part of the client and the provider. That is, some clients may be afraid to see a physician, and some physicians may be fearful of treating some patient types.

Long-Term Care Services

In any population, the need for long-term care more often than not translates into a need for life-sustaining and palliative care. Although the need for long-term care does not reside entirely in the elderly, this subpopulation is the major recipient of this type of care. This characteristic of the population at risk may be the feature that distinguishes their need from the need of those requiring life-sustaining acute care services. If there is any difference at all, it might be said that for a disease condition such as AIDS there is always hope for a cure, but there can never be a cure for old age. This is not to suggest that growing old necessarily brings with it disease conditions or that disease conditions in the elderly cannot be cured, rather that everyone will grow old, and at some point, this often means medical care will be required. To measure the outcomes in this sector, one must turn to the quality-of-life measures. Hospice and palliative care surely must be judged to have adequately addressed the need of this vulnerable population if individuals can live pain-free and die with dignity.

We have seen how all types of medical care could theoretically be embraced by our model. But, does the model serve any useful purpose? Even if it is generalizable to all medical services, is it anything more that just a picture? We can answer this question by considering some health care policy decisions, by locating their focus point in the model, and then by tracing the possible effects throughout the system.

Health Care Policy

It is not the intent of this text to provide a detailed analysis or chronology of public policy in the United States or Canada because many excellent texts are available (for example, see Jonas 1977; Taylor 1978; Meilicke and Storch 1980; Starr 1982; Frech 1988).

Two major health care policy decisions that immediately spring to mind are the 1965 amendments to the Social Security Act, P.L. 89-97 Title XVLLL (Medicare) and Title XLX (Medicaid). Although many revisions to these policies have been made since their inception in 1965, the main theme of the policies remains: to attenuate the financial barrier to access for two sectors of the population, the elderly and the poor. As such, the focal point in the model was the affordability element of access. There is no question that these policies led to an increase in the demand for care that, to the extent which providers responded, translated into increased utilization.

From our model, we can see that there are other barriers to access for which this legislation was not intended. Without any prescribed corresponding changes in the services available in the system—that is, by increasing resources or reorganizing existing ones—some form of rationing other than price would have to emerge. The manifestation of this was providers refusing to treat patients with the characteristics often associated with these two subpopulations. Duncan and McKinstry (1988) report on the negative consequences for hospitals receiving a large number of economically motivated admissions. Increased utilization, particularly by these two subpopulations, would certainly lead to some reduction in need, but the discovery element of the paradoxical concept would suggest that an increased comfort level in approaching the medical care system could lead to an increase in identified need. We must also take account of the zero-price effect and recognize the potential for an increase in overmet need.

In the Canadian system, all of these concerns apply to the population as a whole since the financial barrier was removed for all citizens. The Canada Health Act of 1983 mandates that all provincial programs will meet the following criteria:

- Comprehensiveness: All medically required services without dollar limits, based solely on demonstrated medical need
- Universality: Available to all residents on uniform terms
- Portability: Applies regardless of client relocation within Canada
- Administration: Single, government-approved payer in each province
- Accessibility: Assure reasonable access (Shah 1990)

The U.S. and Canadian governments, through these policies, serve as the purchasers of care on behalf of their constituents. In this capacity, they are instrumental in determining the price that will be paid for services. The focus of this element of policy decisions is clearly on the organization and productivity component of the model, for it is there, under market conditions, that prices are determined. In fact, government efforts can be seen as setting or agreeing to the market price.

The development and implementation of the diagnosis-related group (DRG)–based prospective payment system (PPS) for reimbursing hospitals (Social Security Amendments of 1983, Title VL) and the resource based relative value scale (RBRVS) (Hsiao et al. 1988) for reimbursing physicians represent an attempt to establish a more realistic price for these services based on the resources required to produce them. There are many variations on these methodologies in the United States and Canada, but an overriding principle prevails: it must establish the relative amount of resources consumed in the generation of the service and pay an amount consistent with the resource intensity.

Our model alerts us to the fact that by controlling price, expenditures can be affected, but not to the same degree as achieved by controlling quantity. Recognizing this, both governments resort to quantity or utilization restriction. In other words, governments receive greater payoffs by reducing the number of individuals eligible and the number of services covered in the benefit package.

This same area of organization and productivity was targeted by HMO legislation (P.L. 93-222, 1973) and all forms of managed care activity. Legislation of this nature was designed to encourage use of the optimum combination of resources in producing services. The HMO model of resource organization was certainly responsible for some dramatic changes in overall expenditures for its enrolled population. This was achieved, however, through the use of standards and protocol rather than any productivity improvement or economies of scale. Simply put, HMOs established fairly rigorous criteria for hospitalization, thereby reducing inpatient care quite dramatically. The criticism leveled at HMOs and some other forms of managed care is that there is an incentive to underserve the enrolled population, which in terms of our model, means unmet need.

Government funding of research represents an intervention focused on identifying need and determining the services required to address that need. Research that probes the frontiers of our current knowledge of disease leads to the discovery of new disease conditions, and clinical trials are a prominent part of the search for the cures.

Legislation directed at monitoring quality has come in the form of the professional review organization (PRO) (Social Security Amendment of 1983, Title VL) policy and its predecessor, the professional standards review organization (PRSO) (P.L. 92-603, 1972). These bodies generally concentrated their efforts on process review (such as patient record audits) and to some extent, on gross outcome measures (such as inpatient death rates). This policy attempted to emphasize the state-of-the-art modifying force and, to a lesser extent, outcomes.

Attempts to address other barriers to access have been made. Policies such as loan forgiveness to medical school graduates who agree to work in a designated underserved area were focused on the accessibility element of access. Policies that encouraged the recruitment of minorities and women into medical school were designed to address, not only the human rights and equity issues, but the acceptability perspective of access. It was expected that by recruiting from certain populations and geographic areas, the graduates would be more likely to return to those areas to practice medicine. If successful, this would improve accessibility.

The focus of much discussion and concern over the years, regional planning produced some successes and some failures. Perhaps an ancestor to medical care planning policies, the Hospital

Survey and Construction Act (1946), or the Hill-Burton Program (P.L. 79-725, 1946), certainly achieved its objective—it was responsible for the construction of nearly 40 percent of acute care beds in the United States, increasing the supply from 3.5 per 1,000 population to 4.5 per 1,000 (Dowling and Armstrong 1980). This addressed not only availability but accessibility.

The Regional Medical Programs (RMP) Act of 1965 (P.L. 89-239), was an attempt to reduce the wide variation in the quality of care in the treatment of the three major death-causing conditions—heart disease, stroke, and cancer. It was designed to encourage voluntary regional cooperation among medical schools, hospitals, and research centers with an intent to facilitate the dissemination of the latest knowledge in the treatment of these conditions. This legislation focused on the modifying element between identified need and services required to satisfy need, the state of the art. State of the art, as presented in Chapter 5, was recognized as a variable condition, contingent on the services and knowledge available in any given area. RMP was, therefore, directed toward an improvement in the state-of-the-art element. According to our model, success in this endeavor would produce a change in the services required to satisfy need. The required change might be an increase or decrease in the number of services or, more likely, a change in the type of service. The act recognized the potential for this effect and made funding available for continuing education and training for physicians.

The Comprehensive Health Planning (CHP) Act of 1967 (P.L. 89-749) was designed to facilitate development of a system of voluntary comprehensive planning agencies responsible for developing state and local plans for personal health care services and environmental health services. Although directed at the organization element in our model, this legislation specified that the planning must be achieved without interfering with the prevailing patterns of medical practice. In addition, the National Health Planning and Resource Development (NHPRD) Act of 1974 (P.L. 93-641) was introduced to pull together the elements of Hill-Burton, RMP, and CHP and to resolve some of the problems encountered by those programs. Bice (1980) quotes the then Secretary of Health, Education and Welfare, Eliot Richardson, as stating that these separate planning functions were "hopelessly confusing and sometimes duplicative and overlapping." It combined the foci and expectations of the three individual programs. Hyman (1976) describes the NHRPD Act as placing emphasis on a consumer-provider partnership, comprehensive planning, regulation, and evaluation. It also provided for a close relationship among regional, state, and federal governments.

Our discussion has just scratched the surface of the many types of medical care service and government interventions. Our purpose was to explore the generalizability and utility of the model developed in this text; students who feel important services or legislation have been omitted are encouraged to challenge the model by fitting them into the model and tracing the impact.

In closing, the intent of this text was to provide a framework of the medical care system. The task was undertaken because of a concern that the burgeoning depth and breadth of the body of knowledge in this field might further fuel the trend of fragmenting the students' understanding. The hope is that the text will whet the appetites for more in-depth studies in all of the areas covered by the conceptual model, and toward that end, students will become familiar with the scholarly sources that inspired this work.

Discussion Questions

1. Select a particular public health care need and test whether the conceptual model can be generalized to that sector of the health care field.

2. Select a particular health care need of the elderly and test whether the model can be generalized to that sector.

3. What impact would the introduction of a health insurance program, funded by general revenue, have on the medical care system? Trace the effect throughout the model.

4. Select a particular piece of health care legislation, place it in context in the model, and trace its effect through the system.

References

Bice, T. W. "Health Services Planning and Regulation." In *Introduction to Health Services*, edited by S. J. Williams and P. R. Torrens, 325–54. New York: John Wiley & Sons, 1980.

Dowling, W. L., and P. A. Armstrong. "The Hospital." In *Introduction to Health Services*, edited by S. J. Williams and P. R. Torrens, 125–68. New York: John Wiley & Sons, 1980.

Duncan, R. P., and A. K. McKinstry. "Inpatient Transfers and Uncompensated Care." *Hospital & Health Services Administration* 33 (Summer 1988): 237–48.

Frech, H. E., III. *Health Care in America: The Political Economy of Hospitals and Health Insurance.* San Francisco: Pacific Research Institute for Public Policy, 1988.

Freeman, H. E., R. J. Blendon, L. H. Aiken, S. Sudman, C. F. Mullinix, and C. R. Corey. "Americans Report on Their Access to Health Care." *Health Affairs* (Spring 1987): 6–18.

Hsaio, W. C., P. Braun, D. Yntema, and E. R. Becker. "Estimating Physicians' Work For a Resource-Based Relative Value Scale." *New England Journal of Medicine* 319 (September 1988): 835–41.

Hyman, H. H. *Health Planning: A Systematic Approach.* Germantown, MD: Aspen Systems Corporation, 1976.

Jonas, S. *Health Care Delivery in the United States.* New York: Springer Publishing Company, 1977.

Meilicke, C. A., and J. L. Storch. *Perspectives on Canadian Health and Social Services Policy: History and Emerging Trends.* Ann Arbor, MI: Health Administration Press, 1980.

Shah, C. P. *Public Health and Preventive Medicine in Canada*, 2d ed. Toronto, Ontario: University of Toronto Press, 1990.

Starr, P. *The Social Transformation of Medicine.* New York: Basic Books, 1982.

Taylor, M. G. *Health Insurance and Canadian Public Policy.* Montreal, Quebec: McGill-Queen's University Press, 1978.

Index

About the Author

Michael J. Long, M.A., Ph.D., is Professor and Director of the Master of Public Health Program at the Wichita State University, Kansas. He has previously held faculty positions at the University of Alberta, Wayne State University, Eastern Michigan University, the Medical University of South Carolina, and Pennsylvania State University.

As part of a research team at the Commission on Professional and Hospital Activities in Ann Arbor, Michigan, Long was a co-principal investigator in the first evaluation of DRG-based PPS for the Health Care Financing Administration (HCFA). The team carried out other major evaluation studies for the Prospective Payment Assessment Commission (ProPAC), the National Institute of Mental Health (NIMH), and the National Association of Childrens Hospitals and Related Facilities (NACHRI). He has authored many articles in national and international peer review journals.

Long has been a faculty consultant in the W.K. Kellogg–sponsored baccalaureate Health Administration project and is a consultant to the Ontario Council on Graduate Studies. He received his master's degree in economics from the University of Oklahoma and his doctorate in medical care organization from the University of Michigan, where he received a National Center for Health Services Research (NCHSR) dissertation grant award.

Other Publications From Health Administration Press

▼▼▼▼▼▼▼▼▼▼▼▼▼▼▼▼▼▼▼

HEALTH POLICY ISSUES:
An Economic Perspective on Health Reform
By Paul J. Feldstein

In this issue-oriented book the author explores topics in healthcare policy from an economic perspective. This book is written primarily for non-economists – both students and professionals – to help them understand the political aspects of financing and delivering health services.

Feldstein, a professor and FHP Foundation Distinguished Chair in Health Care Management at the University of California, Irvine, discusses health policy from the point of view that the most effective solutions to economic problems will be those that continue to rely on market incentives to control costs.

Chapters cover such topics as: the rise in medical expenditures, how much should be spent on medical care, how much insurance should everyone have, rationing of medical services, competition among hospitals, the new Medicare payment system, vertically integrated healthcare organizations and employer mandated national health insurance.

Softbound, 321 pages, September 1994, $34.00,
Order No. 0949, ISBN 1-56793-019-0.
An AUPHA/ HAP Book.

▲▲▲▲▲▲▲▲▲▲▲▲▲▲▲▲▲▲▲▲▲▲

A Health Administration Press Journal

▼ ▼ ▼▼▼▼▼▼▼▼▼▼▼▼▼▼▼ ▼ ▼

FRONTIERS OF HEALTH SERVICES MANAGEMENT

The ideal guide for busy executives, each quarterly issue is a collection of forecasts and perspectives on one of today's emerging healthcare topics. Past issues have discussed regional hospital systems, effective governance in the 1990s, universal health insurance, trends in hospital–physician relationships, future health personnel issues, strategic alliance management, and total quality management.

Subscriptions: $65.00/year in the U.S.; $75.00 in Canada and all other countries. ISSN 0748-8157.

BOOK ORDERING INFORMATION

All Health Administration Press Publications are sent on a 30-day approval. To order call, (708) 450-9952, or send your order to The Foundation of the American College of Healthcare Executives, Order Processing Center, Dept. LO94, 1951 Cornell Avenue, Melrose Park, IL 60160-1001.

JOURNAL SUBSCRIPTION INFORMATION

Health Administration Press offers a money-back guarantee on all journal subscriptions. If you are not completely satisfied, simply write and cancel your subscription, you will receive a refund on all unmailed issues. Multi-year subscriptions are not available.

Please send checks made payable to the name of the publication for subscriptions. Current rates expire on December 31, 1995. Address orders to: The Foundation of the American College of Healthcare Executives, Order Processing Center, Dept. LO94, 1951 Cornell Avenue, Melrose Park, IL 60160-1001. Or for more information, call: (708) 450-9952.

▼ ▼▼▼▼▼▼▼▼▼▼▼▼▼▼▼▼ ▼ ▼